On The Edges Of Anthropology

On The Edges of Anthropology
(Interviews)

James Clifford

PRICKLY PARADIGM PRESS
CHICAGO

© 2003 James Clifford
All rights reserved.

Prickly Paradigm Press, LLC
5629 South University Avenue
Chicago, Il 60637

www.prickly-paradigm.com

ISBN: 0-9728196-0-6
LCCN: 2003110983

Printed in the United States of America on acid-free
paper.

Third Thoughts

Five interlocutors invite me to reflect on different aspects and moments of my work. Their questions provoke a kind of thinking-out-loud: ideas restated and revised, second thoughts. One interviewer is a Brazilian ethnologist who asks about my background as a historian and how I approach the history of anthropology. Another is a British cultural theorist concerned with site-specificity and the "ethnographic" turn in contemporary art. A third brings questions from comparative literature, and a Portuguese perspective on North American identity politics. An anthropologist from Hawai'i elicits my thoughts on decolonization and cultural change in the Island Pacific. A Japanese anthropologist, now working with

Mayans in Guatemala, pursues similar issues in the context of contemporary indigenous struggles.

Interviews can reveal how one's work emerges from particular times and places. Reading these second thoughts now, it's apparent that during the years they address, 1970-2000, profound changes were underway. In the universities, newly diverse populations filled the classrooms; canons came under scrutiny; academic genres and disciplines blurred. And even in the relatively insulated intellectual milieux that I frequented, there was a pervasive sense of being displaced, undermined, provoked by world historical forces: unfinished business from the global "sixties," social movements, new politics of representation and culture, the rise of neo-liberalism, novel forms of empire, communication, government and resistance. Many stop-gap terms registered the changes: "post-modernity," "late capitalism," "globalization," "post-industrial" society, "decolonization," "multicultur-alism," "transnationality," "the world system of cultures"...

We struggle to locate ourselves in a tangle of histories, without benefit of overview or hindsight. There are more things in modernity than are dreamed of by our economics and sociology. Everywhere global forces interact with local and emergent projects to make and remake cultural arrangements, discrepant orders. Teleological, ethno-centric, visions of globalization or development cannot grasp this complexity. We need a more contin-gent, multiply positioned realism. Working the edges of anthropology—self-reflexive, ethnographic and historical—these interviews search for critical openness. Even as, inexorably, they begin to sound rather "late twentieth century"...

I would like to thank my interlocutors, José Reginaldo Gonçalves, Alex Coles, Manuela Ribeiro Sanches, Robert Borofsky, and Yoshinobu Ota, for their generous efforts. I have edited the interviews for republication as a group, adding an example here, sharpening a point there, but never departing from the basic content of the original versions. While eliminating some repetitions, I have allowed important topics to recur, to ramify, in different exchanges.

These interviews originally appeared in the following places:

1. *Boletim da ABA* (Associação Brasileira de Antropologia) No 25, March 1996, pp. 6-11. (In Portugese)
2. "An Ethnographer in the Field." *Site-Specificity: The Ethnographic Turn*, Alex Coles, ed. *De-, dis-, ex*. (London: 2000) No. 4, 52-71.
3. "The Art of Tacking." *Etnográfica* (Lisbon: 2000) 4 (2): 371-388.
4. "Valuing the Pacific." *In Remembrance of Pacific Pasts*. Robert Borofsky, ed. Honolulu: University of Hawaii Press, 2000: 92-101.
5. Afterword to Japanese translation of *The Predicament of Culture*, 2003. Kyoto: Jimbun Shoin. (In Japanese)

1. Interviewer: José Reginaldo Gonçalves Rio de Janeiro, December 1994

RG: I could start by asking how you became a historian.

JC: By chance—or so it seems now. In college, I took a course, got a good grade, and continued. But when I was in graduate school it became clear that I wasn't going to be a "real" historian, because I was too interested in anthropology and literature. At Harvard I did some teaching in the History and Literature program and found myself more attracted to the literary texts than to the historical ones. Meanwhile I got interested in anthropology because I had a girlfriend who was an anthropologist. There were also, of course—or so it seems in retrospect—intellectual reasons.

An important book for me in graduate school, where I was studying modern European social and intellectual history, was Raymond Williams' *Culture and Society* (1958). It showed me a way of talking about ideas like "culture" and "art" not simply at the level of intellectual influences, but as complex responses entangled with historical processes: the legacy of the French Revolution, mass democracy, the Industrial Revolution. Williams saw ideas as complex social responses in a way I wasn't used to seeing in intellectual history. *Culture and Society* brilliantly historicized the idea of culture in its more literary or humanist versions. But there was a major strand of the idea that it didn't discuss: the anthropological or ethnographical notion. At the end of the nineteenth century, culture was still generally thought of in the singular: people had higher or lower degrees of culture. It was a very important change when it became possible to say "cultures" in the plural—a specific moment, in English at least, toward the end of the nineteenth century. I thought that what Williams had done for the humanist and literary culture idea maybe I could do for the ethnographical and anthropological version. I'd explore its continuity with and difference from the humanist idea, adding a historical context that Williams didn't develop in *Culture and Society*: the colonial situation. That has remained a fundamental background for my work as a historian, and I suppose a critic, of anthropology. The important change, the historical hinge, has always been the uneven process of decolonization, becoming global in scope after World War II and gathering force in the sixties. I have tracked the decentering of European authority and of certain modes of work and rhetoric in anthropology in that historical conjuncture.

RG: Were you particularly influenced by some French or British historian?

JC: The new model for writing social and cultural history was, of course, E. P. Thompson's *The Making of the English Working Class* (1963). It was a really moving book, especially for our politicized sixties generation, and a number of my friends who became social historians went that way. I remained committed to being an intellectual historian in some form, trying—as I've said—to do for the anthropological culture idea what Williams had done in *Culture and Society*. It was a time when historical and ethnographic styles were beginning to come together. I remember the revelation of reading Thompson's essay called "Time, Work, Discipline and Industrial Capitalism," where he talks about how time was experienced and measured before and after "factory time." He quotes Evans-Pritchard on how the Nuer use measures such as "pissing time," a rather relative standard. And he shows how seasonal, diurnal, physical intervals and cycles were rationalized in the process of training men, women, and children for industrial work. These are the kinds of issues that any anthropologist would immediately recognize, but I was getting them through a form of social/cultural history. It's an interesting and ongoing question for me how much anthropology E.P. Thompson had read. Some to be sure. I've been interested in how anthropological ideas travel in the disciplines. How are they translated and blocked? Why, for example, was there so little direct influence by British social anthropology on the development of "cultural studies," at least in the U.K.?

RG: Your first book is *Person and Myth* (1982). It's a work about Maurice Leenhardt. Why and how did you come to choose it?

JC: More chance. In a way the project chose me. As a graduate student I was awarded a traveling fellowship to work on the history of anthropology in France and Britain. I still thought I was going to do a rather classical intellectual history: you know, pick three prominent figures, maybe in three national traditions, and write a chapter or two on each. I think my research proposal focused on Malinowski, Boas, Durkheim, something like that. Rather naïve: and anyway, George Stocking was in England at that time researching what would become *Victorian Anthropology*, and he sort of colonized that area. He was very helpful to me, but it was perfectly clear that he was way ahead, and this was his turf. So I ended up focusing on French anthropology.

RG: When was that?

JC: Mid-'70s. I went to Europe with the lineage in my head that we all knew in the United States:

Durkheim—Mauss—Lévi-Strauss. But when I got to France I found there was much more to French anthropology than that, and I started to discover a world of other people, some of whom I've written about. Leenhardt was a kind of chance occurrence really; I had never heard of him, I hardly knew where New Caledonia was. But I was working in the library of the Musée de L'Homme, which is one of the few libraries that has any open shelves, where you can browse. I was looking for something about Lévy-Bruhl, and I glanced along the shelf—one of my best "methods" of research. Beside the thing I was looking for there was a set of essays in homage to Maurice Leenhardt. So I took it back to my desk, thinking: "Hum…. This is interesting…. The French were supposed not to have done intensive fieldwork. Leenhardt must be the exception that confirms the rule." He did long-term ethnography, but as an evangelist, only later becoming a professional ethnologist. I thought Leenhardt would make an interesting digression—perhaps part of one chapter. Well, after almost two years, at the very end of my stay in Paris, Leenhardt's son heard through the grapevine that I was interested in his father and invited me to lunch. Raymond Leenhardt presented me with a large pile of transcribed letters his father had written in New Caledonia, from about 1902 until 1926 (when he was forced out of the colony). I said: "But I can't read all these letters, I'm leaving Paris next week." He said: "Take them home. I have a copy." I spent a whole summer reading and was trapped. The digression became a whole book: a fascinating, exemplary story.

To understand the letters I got out the maps, to follow Leenhardt, valley by valley; and I read up on New Caledonia's colonial history.

This unexpected project turned out to be very valuable, because it allowed me to see the production of anthropological knowledge in a concrete colonial situation: the ugly, complicated, and ambivalent power relations this missionary-ethnographer was struggling within and against, that both limited and empowered him as a historical subject. Leenhardt died in 1954 just as the anti-colonial movement in France was heating up, and so his life was circumscribed by the heyday of imperialism. Within this particular moment, he was considered to be a radical. But seen from post-colonial or decolonizing perspectives, he seems a liberal, someone implicated in the system. Situating Leenhardt historically allowed me to see how radical/liberal knowledge within a colonial situation was complexly determined. Leenhardt was in many ways a critic of colonialism, but he was also very much part and parcel of the milieu he worked in. So I was being forced to contextualize his relativistic knowledge in a very concrete way: good training for an intellectual historian becoming a cultural historian.

In retrospect I can also see a more personal agenda. Leenhardt's life showed me the limits of a certain ideological horizon—in his case very broad—a kind of liberal Protestant, syncretic vision. He came to recognize, and to accept, the Word of God taking exotic forms, some of them very strange for a European. Historicizing this vision helped me to see the limits of a monotheistic spirituality seriously grappling with alterity, which for Leenhardt meant traditional Melanesian socio-mythic forms rooted in a specific terrain. His work was an exercise in creative religious translation and also a confrontation with the limits of translation. I was raised in a free-thinking Protestant milieu, an ecumenical, almost deist family. What were my limits, the limits of a universalizing, progressive ecumenism? I am not a believing Christian, but my liberal humanist subjectivity has been structured by Christianity. I had to confront that. And I also had to wrestle a bit with the assumptions of the biographical genre I had adopted, the Western conceptions of the self that were built into it.

RG: How would you describe the difference between your work as a historian of anthropology and the work of people like George Stocking?

JC: George Stocking is the premier historian of anthropology, and his work is extremely complex and deep. I'm a historical critic of anthropology, one might say. And while I hope there's a real sense of historical context and location in what I do, I don't do the kind of archival work Stocking does. The Leenhardt book comes closest. Stocking has been an important influence and alter-ego. He was very encouraging to me, a younger scholar, and I have depended on his work. But as historical accounts of anthropology our works differ in how we define our "object." Stocking basically takes the broad range of definitions by anthropologists of their field—a contested domain—and then writes the history of that domain as a very full intellec-

tual and institutional history. In addition to tracing the
lives and works of prominent anthropologists he
investigates funding sources and practices like fieldwork and travel. His goal is a rich cultural history of
the discipline in its various contexts—as anthropologists have defined themselves. There's a way in which
Stocking is, from the standpoint of anthropologists,
"our historian." And I don't mean to imply that he's
captured by "his people." He works hard to keep his
distance. But he's close to professional anthropologists
in a way that fieldworkers are to their hosts. He works
within an anthropology department, at the University
of Chicago, a "central" location in the discipline.

I'm more marginal to the field. I frequent the
borders. And that's my basic methodological principle,
if one could call it that: Never accept, never take as a
beginning or ending point, what the discipline says it
is. Ask instead: What do anthropologists, for all their
disagreements, say they are *not*? Then focus on the
historical *relationship* that is being policed, or negotiated—the process of "disciplining" that goes on at the
edge. There are a lot of ongoing, perhaps unresolv-
able, internal debates within anthropology. For
example, I think the question of culture vs. biology, an
argument with a long history, is internal to the field.
An opposition to "nature" is built into the idea of
"culture." There are also perennial issues such as: how
much like natural science and how much like history
are we? And how much like sociology? Questions
recur about anthropology as a hyphenated discipline,
worries about the field's fundamental identity. These
are normal, "internal" arguments and negotiations.

But other, more absolute, statements of what anthropologists are *not*, more categorically define the disciplinary community, its habitus, and I have tended to position my work on those borders.

One such border is marked by the non-negotiable statement: "We're not missionaries." But the book about Maurice Leenhardt deals with a missionary who can't be distanced in that way. Like all borders the boundary is, in practice, both crossed and maintained. Another disciplinary edge: "We're not colonial officers." We're not here to rule. And a third constitutive "no": "We're not travelers or travel writers." Three important, changing, frontiers. When anthropologists say "we're not missionaries," they may be asserting: "missionaries change the culture, we don't." Yes and no. There's a blindness in the insight, in the process of taking a position "outside" culture-contact and change. Elements of cultural interaction may be marginalized or hidden by the self-location which says "we're not part of the changes." Indeed, during much of the twentieth century missionaries may have been less likely than anthropologists to reify an "ethnographic present," a static, pre-contact, traditional culture. Missionaries—some of them at least—were more likely to be interested in matters of syncretism and cultural process. That's certainly true of Leenhardt, for whom change *is* culture, culture *is* syncretism.

Now, for all these "we are not" statements there's currently a kind of return of the repressed going on. Cultural contact, change, religious conversion, etc. are no longer the disruptive, constitutive outsides of anthropological authenticity. The second claim: "we are not colonial officers" says, in effect, "we are not part of the colonial system, we are scientists, liberals, who preserve our critical independence." Again, yes and no. We are all familiar, now, with critiques of anthropology as, not exactly a tool of colonialism, which is much too simple, but as a set of practices embedded in a context of power, part of a system. These critiques, and the often disconcerting hostility to "anthros" by mobilized natives, show that anthropology has, indeed, played a role in colonial situations, whether consciously or not. For example, one is now struck by the not-so-simple fact of Evans-Pritchard going to the Nuer—who didn't want him there and who had quite recently been the object of a punitive military expedition—and surviving. Evans-Pritchard writes quite frankly about this in the Introduction to *The Nuer*: he is unwelcome; at first no one but the kids will speak to him. The question is: "why was he not killed?" Well, when white people go into situations of that sort—and this is true of many of the places anthropologists have worked—there's a prior history of pacification. The locals have understood the message: don't harm white folks, because if you do many more of your own people will suffer. The anecdote points to a historical location, often based on white skin privilege, that guarantees an important degree of safety. The statement "we are not colonial officers" is a way of positioning oneself as marginal to the colonial regime, in a place of relative innocence which is itself a position within an unequal field of power relations. I've written about that in several places, especially concerning ethnographic liberals like Leenhardt, Marcel Griaule, Michel Leiris and others, pointing to a rather complex history of anthropology in colonial contexts. As with the missionary frontier, there's a crossing and policing of roles, a history of changing border relations.

And the third disciplinary edge: "We are not travel writers." What's thrown out of anthropology with travel and travel writing is, of course, the "literary," and with it the "subjective." Literary representation is personal, embodied, rhetorical. It's that place where people talk about their feelings; they use the first person singular a lot; their bodies are visible, present. Think of all the discomforts, the sensual perceptions of the traveler—very different from those of the field worker, who in the classic ethnographies becomes invisible in the text, at least after the preface. This is all in question now. What is sometimes called "reflexivity" or "experimentalism" in current ethnographic writing—which can involve more use of the first person singular, more explicit use of rhetorical or literary devices, more attention to the writing of anthropology—all these trends can be understood as a kind of return of that expelled "travel writer." Travel writers typically pass through situations quickly and thus lack the fieldworker's depth of perspective. But the border can become fuzzy. Some travelers stay a long time and their accounts may say more about race and power relations than ethnographies focused on culture and social structure. They may reveal more of the capital city, and the technology of how one gets to a "field," than texts like Malinowski's *Argonauts of the*

Western Pacific which says about his arrival in the Trobriands simply, "imagine yourself sat down on a beach." Dreamlike. How did he get to that beach? The travel writer will tell you about the boat, the missionary airplane, or the Land Rover. The ethnographer classically will not—you are dropped in. I've been interested in working on the ways that various practices and rhetorics of "travel literature" are held at bay (and sometimes unofficially invoked) by an ethnography that in the twentieth century struggles to define itself as a science, which means defining the field as a site of controlled, "deep," interactive research.

In recent years what was kept out by distancing the travel writer is returning. This is not to say that anthropology is only travel (or evangelism or colonial power), but to say that the border is being renegotiated. In this perspective, the book *Writing Culture*, which involved bringing into view literary and rhetorical practices in ethnography, remakes the worldly border with travel and travel writing.

RG: How do you describe the effects of these kinds of questions on the American anthropological community? What about the consequences of these questions?

JC: Books like *Writing Culture* and *The Predicament of Culture* have been part of a ferment, part of something already going on, that has, I think, significantly changed anthropological practices. Certainly those works did not introduce some new paradigm, the "postmodern anthropology" people sometimes love to hate. But the books, and the ferment that made them possible, did raise a set of critical questions that remain on the agenda of cross-cultural representation.

RG: How has this work been received by anthropologists?

JC: To speak personally, my writing has been warmly received in some quarters, and violently rejected in others. Its appeal may not always have been for the best reasons. For example, I suspect that more than a few anthropologists are writers or novelists, *poètes manqués*. They have a novel filed away somewhere. So, when one says "really what you are doing is like literature," there's a kind of too easy assent: "Oh yes, that's right! Writing ethnography is like writing a novel." But that was only a very small part of the message. The "literariness" of anthropology that was being raised in *Writing Culture* was more like that which someone like Hayden White ascribes to historical discourse: the tropological pre-encoding of "the real," the rhetorical constitution of facts at the very level of their facticity. What phenomena emerge from the plenitude, the overabundance of things that could be considered facts? And how do they emerge as already narrated, already historicized objects, through the processes of rhetorical condensation and narrative arrangement? Facts come already narrated, and then are re-narrated in the process of conscious interpretation. This strong version of "literariness" is a threat to many concepts of scientific objectivity, and so *Writing*

Culture was accused of "hyper relativism," "nihilism," and (a favorite) "navel gazing." That's because in this view, once a certain centrality is given to rhetoric, once recognition is accorded to the positioned subject in a discourse, and once processes of representation become constitutive of socio-cultural life, the result is defined as a "subjective reality." In these responses I see deployed a kind of objective/subjective machine, a sorting device for parsing things according to a sharp ontological dichotomy. But most discourses occupy intermediate positions along a continuum. The objective/subjective machine works to keep things clear. For example, in recent decades the machine has been attuned to how the first person singular is used in a text. If you transgress a certain (invisible) line, you may suddenly find yourself relegated to the "subjective" side. When and where, exactly, the parsing takes place I find rather intriguing. As a relative outsider to anthropology, I wonder why certain personal, poetic, or narrative moves are suddenly seen as "merely subjective," or "self-absorbed" while others remain within the proper domain of science.

But at the same time that these, and other, defensive reactions have been deployed, there has been a positive response. In practice there's been a selective appropriation by various people of elements of the critique. This is happening from a lot of directions. People take certain elements and combine them with other projects. Feminist anthropology, for example, has been both resisting and borrowing critically from books like *Writing Culture*.

RG: How would you describe the relationship between "cultural studies" and anthropology in the U.S.?

JC: That's a borderland I've been crossing a lot recently. A lot of exciting work is going on. But let me just focus on the question of disciplinary identity. The heterogeneity of anthropology is well known. If you look at the range of contemporary departments, it can be hard to imagine that these are part of the same discipline. There is a crisis in the field. I think it is a positive crisis, on balance, but like all crises it leaves people anxious about borders and about disciplining. An everyday example: Suppose you are asked to teach a graduate seminar introducing the field of socio-cultural anthropology. What do you include? I keep an eye out for what goes into those courses, and it varies enormously. For some there would be no question but that Marx has to be there. Marx is not an anthropologist. But there is a strand of current anthropology in which the relation of culture and political economy is crucial, for example, the work of Eric Wolf, William Roseberry, etc. We might ask "is Radcliffe-Brown essential in this course?" Thinking about a course forces you to prioritize, because you may only have fifteen weeks or less. Do kinship studies have to be represented? Lewis Henry Morgan? Does Meyer Fortes have to be there—and the early Lévi-Strauss? And what if this means not having space for Simone de Beauvoir? If you include Lévi-Strauss, why not de Beauvoir, a founding figure in feminist discourses which have played a crucial role in postwar anthro-

pology? How choose between Weber and Saussure?
Fanon or Foucault? And so on.

Where does anthropology begin? Look at the
disciplinary histories. Sometimes they start with Plato
and the Greeks. Many begin with the birth of
European rationality: some in the Enlightenment,
some earlier. Others like Robert Lowie in his *History
of Ethnological Theory* give centrality to fieldwork, and
so begin with early travelers. The strategies vary a lot.
In practice, one can't build one's introductory course
around an agreed canon. Does one have to include
some feminist or postcolonial theory? Doesn't one
have to have some semiotics? Can one really do
without a certain range of literary theory or
psychology? Can one bypass political economy? social
history? cognitive science? Can one really do without
gay and lesbian studies, now that questions of sexuality
are emerging in ethnographic and anthropological
work? I could go on. In practice, people usually
compromise by invoking a few founding fathers (and
sometimes now mothers), and then they focus on what
they think is most relevant today. There are many ad
hoc solutions. But the problem of inclusion is a
symptom of the way that anthropology, which was
always an interdisciplinary field, is now awash in interdisciplinarity. The question becomes a rather crucial
one: what's still distinctive about the discipline?

There are many anthropology departments
that are much closer, in most of what they do, to social
and cultural history. Would it be enough to say: "We
write the social history of places where we go and do
fieldwork." Here fieldwork remains perhaps the last

distinctive element. But considering the range of what cultural anthropologists actually do, including archival work, how exactly are they different? Cultural anthropology used to have a special object, the "primitive"—those folks *out there* or *down there* and *back then*: exotic societies, folklore, rural society, lower classes, etc. But now anthropologists study everything, from tribes to physics labs.

Anthropology used to have a defining paradigm, "culture." But now everybody talks about culture, and it's hard for anthropology to claim openly what they sometimes do informally. "We are the ones who properly understand culture, unlike those literary types." It's not hard to dismiss literary criticism as superficial, as not having the depth and complexity that fieldwork gives. It's more difficult to dismiss "cultural studies" which has its own ethnographic tradition: the Birmingham Center for Contemporary Cultural Studies, the British tradition, which did ethnographies of urban subcultures, youth cultures, music, etc. Is it ethnographic *enough*? Is it *real* fieldwork? This has become an important defining issue for anthropology. The discipline doesn't have the primitive or the exotic other; it doesn't have culture, a paradigm it claims as its own; it doesn't have "Man," that mythic telos, unifying, somehow (at least in America) the rather arbitrary "four fields": archaeology, linguistic anthropology, socio-cultural and physical anthropology. "Man," a science of man, seems like a kind of weird anachronism now—after Foucault, after feminism. It makes no sense anymore as a telos, as an end point for what we are all doing in this discipline. So that's gone too, along with the "primitive" object and the "cultural" paradigm.

What's left? I've already suggested that one can't appeal to an accepted canon of exemplary texts. So we are left with a distinctive research practice. Fieldwork is itself under considerable discussion, because it's much less clear how you define a "field" and what it means to "go into" the field. Indeed, lots of people in many contexts are doing work that can be defined as "ethnographic." But *fieldwork* is, arguably, a special kind of ethnography, a spatial practice of intensive, interactive research organized around the serious fiction of a "field." This site is not so much a discrete, single place as a set of institutionalized practices, a professional habitus. What counts as fieldwork is a rather large can of worms these days, and there's a lot of leeway in practice. But in the U.S., at least, it remains a critical norm that gets deployed in defining moments such as when a graduate student develops a thesis project, or in hiring and firing. In many departments, even the most interdisciplinary ones, the pressure to do something called "real fieldwork" is strong. How long? With whom? Which languages to use and how well? How do you circumscribe your place of work? There are many grey areas to negotiate. And suppose you are a person who wants to study his or her own community? An "indigenous ethnographer." That project may not count, because fieldwork remains linked to distancing, a history of travel, a history of the spatial practice of going *out* to a field in some way. Fieldwork can't be "homework." But how is the crucial distance defined and negotiated, how is it understood? How is this displacement negotiated when the field might be just down the street, when you may go in and out of your field on the subway? All of this is being hammered out in anthropology departments in ways that are still unclear. Anthropological ethnography is a site of negotiation, reinvented traditions, creativity, and disciplining. And for now at least, fieldwork remains an important border marker vis-à-vis "cultural studies," a fluid interdisciplinary formation that potentially shares everything else with socio-cultural anthropology. Indeed, even that mark of difference is in danger of disappearing, dissolving into a more general range of research practices and representational styles. So I see this as a site of creative border crossing and also of intense disciplining. I try to follow these processes as someone recently associated with "cultural studies" who has worked in the borderlands of anthropology.

RG: How would you describe the relationship between the so called "First World" and "Third World" anthropologists? I mean French, British, American anthropologists, and Brazilian, Indian, African anthropologists, etc. How do you describe this kind of field?

JC: The relationships you're describing are emergent ones, and very important. I feel, actually, not well located to map a changing terrain, because I work within the Eurocenter—in a somewhat marginal place, but definitely within the Eurocenter. It's evident that voices, analyses, interpretations, theories are now challenging and displacing "Western" anthropology. These challenges are coming from other centers of work and from differently positioned scholars— whether they want to be called "anthropologists" or not. In a way, the matter of definition isn't crucial for me, because I think anthropology is not a field whose sources, audience or interlocutors are solely or primarily anthropologists or should be. In recent years, important issues have been raised around the problematic figure of the so-called "indigenous anthropologist," a perhaps already outmoded term which marks a moment both of contestation and assimilation. In any event, we are no longer speaking of simple "natives," a term that suggests a pure indige- nous "inside," the reflex of a certain authority of the "outside." It used to be accepted that real anthropolo- gists were "outside" and informants or local historians "inside." That inside/outside relation has been exploded in practice, and the "indigenous anthropolo- gist" is turning out to be something complicated and *multiply located* with respect to the sites of study, of intellectual production and reception. But the ques- tion of who would get to be called an "anthropolo- gist," and who would *want* to be called an anthropolo- gist, thus contending with or contributing to "proper" anthropological knowledge, is a big question which has very much to do with colonial, post- and neo- colonial histories and institutional arrangements in different countries. What are the actual arrangements, who are the audiences for anthropology located in New Delhi, located in Suva, for example, at the University of the South Pacific, or in a place like

Buenos Aires? I am not evading your crucial question when I say that I don't think I'm well placed to answer. It's really a moment, now, in which I need to listen more than to talk.

RG: How would you connect all these questions about disciplinary borders and disciplining with the ongoing social and political debates in the United States since the '80s about monoculturalism and multiculturalism?

JC: Well, there's no doubt that the authority of many disciplines to talk about marginalized peoples is contested to an unprecedented degree. Members of those cultures or societies are saying, publicly: "it is not enough for you to give us voice, to represent us, we wish to represent ourselves in the academy." Anthropology, which for so long spoke for difference, is caught up in, challenged by, the process by which the academy in the U.S.—and it is an uneven process—is becoming more diverse. What's at stake is the inclusion of people of diverse historical back-grounds, people who have been racialized differently and kept in subaltern social positions. Moreover, I would underline the major impact that women, and feminist perspectives, have had in my context. We sometimes forget how male-dominated the academy has been since the medieval university, how recent the emergence of a critical mass of women is. All of these changes, these multiplications of what my colleague Donna Haraway named "situated knowledges," under-mine the ability of disciplines to naturalize their knowledges. Authority is fundamentally contested.

When Evans-Pritchard wrote *The Nuer* he knew exactly who his audience was and it was the "common room," it was those who would be admitted to the university world. He didn't have to worry about Nuer intellectuals reading over his shoulder. Now every anthropologist has to think about that, and it makes a profound difference. I'm certainly not saying that the Native is always right, that inside authority is better than outside authority. All you have to do is to think about your own society, your own limited ability to generalize within your society, to realize that's far too simple. What has been going on—and that I have worked in the midst of—is a kind of repositioning of authorities: not exactly replacing or contradicting authorities, but negotiating new forms of *differential authority*. The current crossing and policing of disciplinary borders is part of this crisis—with the sense of anxiety, of being displaced, that many of us feel. One of the reasons I am so interested in anthropology, and continue to study it after my fashion, is that anthropology has been unusually exposed, publicly vulnerable, in this area. It's a discipline where decolonization had to make a difference, questioning and repositioning virtually all academic practices. Anthropology is exemplary, I think, in struggling to transform its objects and modes of authority...unfinished, open-ended transformations.

2. Interviewer: Alex Coles
London/Santa Cruz, Fall 1999.

AC: Three main factors have made your work vital to debates around art over the last decade and a half. First is your critique of the 1985 Primitivism exhibition at the New York Museum of Modern Art, published in *Art in America*. Second is your interest in the activities of dissident Surrealists such as Bataille and Leiris and perhaps Benjamin too. And third is the way you fore-ground methods of textuality in the book you co-edited, *Writing Culture* (1986). In many ways your writing in the early 1980s prompted the fascination with ethnography in art practice and criticism (firstly by Craig Owens, and more recently by, amongst others, Renée Green and Fred Wilson); in others it draws on it. So, with particular emphasis on the way your work has driven much of the exchange, what do you think of the traffic between art and ethnography? Do you think that it has benefited both sides?

JC: First I'd like to just add one name to your list of quasi-surrealists who inspired me: William Carlos Williams. He was an early, and continuous, influence— a modernist writer who made the choice, against Europe's pull on his generation, for America. And not for New York City, either. For an obscure place, Rutherford, New Jersey, and for the peculiarly inti-mate/distant ethnographic perspective and habitus of a family doctor. His poetic documentary and social critique, mixed with populism, and a visionary streak (vision at ground-level, among real people, their voices and ethnic, gendered, quirky bodies), all this was of great significance for me as a source for an expansive notion of the "ethnographic." Williams' *Paterson* became a model, a provocation for a new kind of realism. This was a situated knowledge, freed from the constraints of scientific objectivity and the Lukacsian "type," a path through even the most particular and subjective facts to a kind of general view, a "big enough" vision.

     It was, perhaps, just the right kind of localism (Williams was, of course, very much in touch with the modernist "centers," Paris and New York) for someone like me in the 1960s and 1970s beginning to feel he was no longer at the progressive center of the world and looking for ways to be off center, but connected. I think this wavering, this fragmenting, of the spatio-temporal centrality of modernism and of "the West" in the '60s (the greater '60s, one might say, following Jameson) has a lot to do with the appeal of "ethno-graphic" dispositions across a wide range of activities. *Writing Culture*, and the writings from the late 1970s and 1980s which were stuck together in *The Predicament of Culture*, were part of a proliferating style.

I was surprised at first by how quickly those two works were taken up by artists, writers, perfor-mance and media people. And I can only situate this influence with reference to a moment in the modernist centers and their satellites when Williams' dicta "no ideas but in things" and "the universal through the particular" took on new kinds of meaning. People no longer saw themselves making "art" or contributing to a cumulative "culture." Art and Culture seemed like local acts now, provincial definitions (an "art-culture system," I called it). And the response wasn't to rush to some new, emergent, historical center of avant-garde activity. Where was that? The world seemed to secrete many, divergent, arts and cultures, discrepant moderni-ties. One's task as an "ethnographer" (defined, predom-inantly, as cultural critic, a defamiliariser and juxta-poser) was to mine the museum, in Fred Wilson's terms, to probe the cracks, search for the emergent: Benjamin's messianic time, without any particular messiah.

I think we can see, now, that this was a response to decentering, and perhaps a preliminary millenialism, by people in a historically displaced condition. Not a universal prescription or normative postmodernity. To be sure, the ethnographic disposition partook of a certain privilege, a luxury to explore one's own coming apart, to work with fragments. But I think it would be wrong to reduce this set of critical and quasi-documentary attitudes to a negative stereotype of "postmodernist" relativity and self-absorption. For those representing marginal, or populist, modes of life and expression it offered a place, albeit circumscribed, in the wider, public debates. And for those coming from sites of relative privilege there was, and is, a genuine openness to a broader world of popular and non-Western possibilities and agencies here. I would like to think that, at its best, the "ethnography" which emerged across many fields in the 1980s rejects quick and dirty symptomatic analyses. It reflects a willingness to look at common sense, everyday practices—with extended, critical and self-critical attention, with a curiosity about particularity and a willingness to be decentered in acts of translation.

AC: One thing that you have been slightly brought to task for, at times by those same art critics, particularly Hal Foster in "The Artist As Ethnographer," is the way you loosen up the notion of what an ethnography can be. In other words, you re-define the parameters of what constitutes fieldwork, participant/observation, etc. But are the methodologies of ethnography infinitely expandable? Or do they snap when pushed too far?

JC: Of course all methodologies, which in the interpretive/historical studies are always modes of partial translation, first get you somewhere and then run out of gas. "Ethnography," whether in its strict anthropological or expanded cultural-critical sense, is no exception: it involves recognition and mis-recognition. Hal Foster, reacting against its sometimes uncritical popularity in art practices of the early 1990s, cuts "ethnography" down to size. And in this he's part of a necessary counter-trend. (There have been regular flare-ups, too, in a border war between anthropology and cultural studies over what counts as real ethnography.) But I would caution readers of Hal's several pages (in *The Return of the Real*) on "the new anthropology" that he provides a very truncated account. His direct references to the movement under discussion are limited to a couple of my essays from the early 1980s. And in a common dismissive move, the new anthropology is reduced to textualism and hyper-reflexivity. This freezes a particular moment of what has been a complex, ongoing critique and decentering of cultural representations and relations of power. There's so much more to the ferment in socio-cultural anthropology during the '80s than a (selective) reading of *The Predicament Of Culture* can register.

Even that book's most "textualist," and often-cited, chapter, "On Ethnographic Authority," is a critique of the modes of critical authority Hal properly questions. To see it as reducing everything to text or—a rather different thing—to discourse, slides over the essay's central proposal that anthropology's former "informants" be thought of as "writers." This proposal argues that the space of cultural representations is populated by differently situated authorities, producers, not simply conduits, of self-reflexive "cultural" knowledge. For there is no longer a standpoint from which one can claim to definitively administer, or orchestrate, the textualization of "identity," "tradition," or "history." A heteroglot, overlapping and contested public culture—including indigenous writers, readers, and performers—characterizes the post-/neo-colonial context which the self-critical work of the late '70s was beginning to reflect, in Western academic contexts. By the late 1980s it was inescapable that anthropological fieldwork would never again be a matter of an outsider scholar interrogating insider natives and emerging with neutral, authoritative knowledge. The "textual" critique of older, classic ethnographies showed that there had always been more going on: more negotiation, translation, appropriation. But now the politics and the poetics were in the open—not only because of the new theoretical self-reflexivity, poststructural concepts of textual indeterminacy and dialogism, but more profoundly because of pressures from decolonisation and feminism.

The chapter in *The Predicament of Culture* on Marcel Griaule was centrally focused on the colonial context, seen from the post-war perspective of its contestation, and emphasizing the issue of African agency in a negotiated ethnographic co-production spanning four decades. The book's later sections critiquing modernist primitivism and the history of collections were equally focused on bringing into view the socially and politically fraught nature of cross-cultural representations. And so expanding the range of activities qualified as ethnographic, or as art/culture-collecting, was an attempt to decenter canonical Western styles. And if this was all done from within a changing "West," and with theoretical tools of self-critique, it was done with an ear out for non-Western, and partially-Western, voices.

Routes, a 1990s book, assumes this mix of location and receptivity, tracking the conjoined practices of travel and translation. It assumes that while one's geo-political, worldly itineraries and encounters are power-fully constrained they are not ultimately determined. Location isn't a prison; it's comprised of material, but unfinished, maps and histories. In this book the ethno-graphic trope is replaced by a "travel" metaphor—simi-larly a source of insight and blindness, a translation term that needs to be cut down to size. Displacement, forced and voluntary, exists in an always-unresolved dialectic with different forms of dwelling, of staying put. Clearly this all has to do with the phenomena too hastily gathered under the rubric of "globalization," a matter of transnational flows, the making and remaking of cultures and places. *Routes* argues against closures in our struggle to understand the present historically. The structuring context of "late capi-talism" troubles (but does not erase) the context of decolonization that organized *The Predicament of Culture*. *Routes* tries to inhabit a tension, an antinomy, of neo- and post-colonial narratives.

AC: In recent years there has been a resurgence of interest in artists who developed an understanding of an ethnographic site in their practices in the late 1960s (particularly Robert Smithson and Lothar Baumgarten). Today the notion of the ethnographic site is being further expanded by a number of artists. This is interesting given that a grasp of site-specificity has always been crucial for ethnographic fieldwork and textual ethnographies. Indeed, in "On Ethnographic Surrealism" you attest to the fact that "exploration of ethnographic activity" must always be set in "specific cultural and historical circumstances." Is this a definition of an ethnographic understanding of site-specificity?

JC: It's interesting to connect an "ethnographic" approach with "site-specificity" in art. Both are ways of decentering established centers of art/cultural production and display, and so I would be tempted to locate them in the general context I've just outlined. But it's important to recognize that turns to the specific and the local occur in contexts of "complex connectivity," to adopt John Tomlinson's substitute for the diffusionist term "globalization." I'd always want to stress, as in the case of *Paterson*, the entanglement of the particular, not with Williams' modernist "universal," but with networks of power and communication. If this means we can no longer speak of the "merely" local, then we need to interrogate the performative specificity of any ethnographic or site-specific production. Such productions make sense only given audience access (physical access, or written, photographic representations). People have to know, somehow, about Spiral Jetty, or Lothar Baumgarten placing the names of Indian groups in a Caracas botanical garden, or Ana Mendieta burning her body's outline on the earth. Nowadays a video camera is an integral part of any site-specific, or local, performance, whether it's Guillermo Gomez-Peña and Coco Fusco infiltrating major museums as caged New World "savages" or the opening of a tribal museum in Alaska. The same goes for any ethnographic work, always already caught up in modes of representation and reception. I suppose that's still *Writing Culture*'s message: we are talking about concrete, relational, articulations of "specificity."

You suggest that something similar applies to temporal contextualizations. The cultural and historical circumstances of "ethnographic surrealism" were, I argued, a Europe putting itself together after a war of unprecedented scale and brutality, and a modernism whose access to the non-Western "primitive" was going through quantitative and qualitative shifts. "Ethnographic surrealism" named a critical formation which made sense in this conjuncture—not an avant-garde method or a precursor of postmodernism. But by recognizing and naming it, I was positioning myself and my readers in the culturally-decentered, corrosively self-critical, post-'60s. Specificity, whether of site or historical moment is always relative to its representations. A local formation, or a temporal conjuncture, is part of some larger projection of relevance or meaningfulness which makes sense in "contact relations" which are never transparent or free of appropriation. This is the basic performativity which an ethnographic poetics and politics assumes.

AC: In your writing you often take the ethnographer (and the discourse of anthropology) as your primary site. A neat quote from Paul Rabinow attests to this, "Clifford takes as his natives, as well as his informants, anthropologists." (You even quoted this passage in *The Predicament of Culture*.) What do you think of if? Is it less true now than it was a decade ago?

JC: Well, my relations to anthropologists, whom I have never considered to be "my natives," have been complex. A kind of fraught, shifting colleagueship would be more like it. Paul's quip was meant to say that I couldn't, as a critic, escape the structures of authority I analyzed in anthropological fieldwork. To which I responded, by making his text an epigraph: "of course." Nor were the predicaments I thought I could see with special clarity in a changing anthropology peculiar to one discipline. But socio-cultural anthropology—perhaps because of a certain historical exposure, because it was so inescapably located in changing (decolonizing, recolonizing, modernizing, re-localizing, etc.) cross-cultural domains—lived through crucial problems of authority in a very public way. And anthropology's experience, its "crisis," became a paradigm for other fields where similar pressures were being felt.

I think that anthropology has grappled with the historical changes in its relations with its "objects" of study in a generally positive way. The process has not led, as some feared, to self-absorption and hyper-relativism, but to much more complex historical accounts of an expanded range of socio-cultural phenomena. As I've already suggested, the occasions of ethnography have come to be articulated in ways that necessarily include discrepant and ongoing processes of cultural representation and reception. Given these developments in socio-cultural anthropology, I find myself now more a participant than an observer. I particularly value the textured perspectives from geo-political "peripheries" and "marginal" places that anthropological ethnography still delivers. The discipline offers a critical corrective to global-systemic projections of the planet and its future. I'm always astonished and chagrined to find how little ethnography and ethnographic history people in the academy and art world at large actually know. (Some read me— or Johannes Fabian's *Time and the Other*, but never his many ethnographies—and think that's all they need.) I keep running into sophisticated scholars, artists, and intellectuals who still assume that the spread of McDonalds in many world cities, or the arrival of English, Coke, country music, anthropology and tourists in places like New Guinea results somehow automatically in a wholesale destruction of local affiliations, a homogenized world culture. Cross-cutting agencies, and the contradictions of everyday life, just disappear. Such a partial, Eurocentric view...and so satisfyingly tragic!

AC: In your most recent book, *Routes*, you develop the idea that a site is not necessarily defined by fixed spatial and temporal boundaries. Specifically, you suggest that a site can be a "contact zone;" i.e. a place located between fixed points, one that is constantly mobile. How did you arrive at this expanded definition?

JC: "Contact zone" is, of course, derived from Mary Louise Pratt's *Imperial Eyes*. She adapts the term from sociolinguistics, the notion of "contact languages" (pidgins and creoles which emerge in specific historical conjunctures) as well as from the work of Fernando Ortiz on "transculturation." These are perspectives that do not see "culture contact" as one form progressively, sometimes violently, replacing another. They focus on relational ensembles sustained through processes of cultural borrowing, appropriation, and translation—multidirectional processes. And if the productions of modernity are exchanges, in this perspective, they are never free exchanges: the work of transculturation is aligned by structural relations of dominance and resistance, by colonial, national, class, and racial hierarchies. Nonetheless, a "contact zone" can never be reduced to cultural dominance or (more positively) education, acculturation, progress, etc. The concept deflects teleologies. In *Routes* I found it useful to think of museums (and a wide range of heritage, cultural performance sites) as "contact zones" because it opened them up to contestation and collaborative activity. It helped make visible the different agendas— aesthetic, historical, and political—that diverse "publics" bring to contexts of display. The sometimes fraught politics of representation that now trouble museums, particularly those which feature non-Western, tribal, and minority cultures, appeared as part of a long, always unfinished, history. Museums as we know them were integral to the expansive "West," its imperial and national projects. The wholesale movement of exotic collections into "artistic" and "cultural" centers, involved appropriations and translations now being re-inflected, and even, to a degree, reversed. In a contact perspective, which complicates zero-sum relation between "tradition" and "modernity," museums become way stations rather than final destinations.

AC: This is different to the way you discussed museums in the 1980s. Can you flesh out this development in your thinking a little more?

JC: In *The Predicament of Culture* I was primarily concerned with a critique of Western institutions. This took two general forms: 1) questioning modes of authority both in academic ethnography and in artworld contexts such as the Museum of Modern Art's provocative exhibit, "'Primitivism' in Twentieth Century Art;" and 2) looking for counter-discourses such as the "ethnographic surrealist" work of Michel Leiris, or the Caribbean surrealism of Aimé Césaire. The book tried to destabilize Western traditions and discourses from within—though the decolonizing pressures it registered (from without) had already undermined this location and, indeed, any permanent inside/outside border. The career of Césaire, passing through Paris, in and out of the West, makes this clear. Looking back on *The Predicament of Culture* in 1990, I tried, with limited success, to mark some of its locations—by geography, race, and gender—by decomposing and recollaging the "Ethnographic Surrealism" essay.

And I worked to deepen the shift of perspective that was latent in the book's last chapter devoted to the Mashpee Indians' inconclusive "tribal" identity trial. There I had confronted an ongoing New England contact history and a native reality that constantly escaped anthropological "culture" and continuous "history," categories that formed my common sense. Moreover, there was nothing radically nomadic, deterritorialized, or rootless about the Indians who persisted in and around this Cape Cod town. I wasn't portraying "postmodern" prototypes. I was trying to bring my primary audience—enlightened, Western-educated skeptics like me—to a realization that we were missing something: a reality of Native American existence that our received notions of culture and history couldn't grasp. The trial made me a lot more sensitive to indigenous movements with their complex rearticulations of tradition and history. One of the first things I published after *The Predicament of Culture* was an essay comparing "Four Northwest Coast Museums" in Vancouver. Two of these were "tribal" museums/cultural centers. The essay, reprinted in *Routes*, marked a crucial discovery for me. I began to see the museum, that most stodgy and Eurocentric of institutions, as a dynamic, disseminating institution which could take a diversity of forms in particular local/global conjunctures. Of course the critics of "heritage industries" and "identity politics" see this development as a characteristic of the superficial cultural politics of postmodernity.

And I think there's no doubt that a globalizing system of cultural commodification is at work. But it's terribly inadequate to reduce the emerging subaltern and local productions that articulate with museums, cultural centers, and (inescapably) tourism to epiphenomena of a late capitalist, postmodern or "Americanized," world system of cultures.

Tribal museums, a proliferating movement, fulfill distinct, if connected, functions. They often perform heritage for both "insiders" and "outsiders," differently. They are part of markets in native art which are unlike the older, ongoing economies in "primitive art"—exclusively governed by Western taste and distribution. The new "tribal" cultural productions are often significantly under native control. (One thinks of Aboriginal acrylics and video-making.) They are "articulated" (a term I much prefer to "invented") traditions: specific linkages of old and new, ours and theirs, secret and public, partial connections between complex socio-cultural wholes. To perform identity, to play the culture-game, is to be alive in postmodernity. But the terms of this liveliness vary. And it's possible to articulate quite old, non-Western things, through the new languages of culture and identity. If a good deal of this becomes commodified, isn't it capitalist hubris to assume that's the end of the story? A closer, more ethnographic, look at particular sites of heritage collecting and performance than one gets from the political-economy system-atizers often tells an ambiguous, open-ended story. There is, undeniably, a systematic aspect to the proliferating politics of heritage, ethnicity and tourism. But it's a system of worlds in contact rather than a world-system.

Tribal museums/cultural centers, I argued in *Routes*, are innovations in a long history of cultural (re)appropriations—situations of ongoing, but always contested, inequality. My contact perspective also touched on sites of discrepant heritage like Fort Ross (the reconstructed Russian/Alaskan outpost in Northern California), on performed heritage and museum-collecting in highland New Guinea, and on the Mayan ruin and tourist site of Palenque. In each case I tried to focus on histories of acculturation—local, regional, global articulation—rather than on systemically produced, commodified identities and differences. The "world of museums" whose byways I began to follow (not just an expanded "museum world") led me out of places like Paris and New York, modernist centers, and into a range of contemporary sites that can't be rounded up historically under the stop-gap language of "posts."

AC: In *Routes* you devote an entire "experimental" chapter to the Susan Hiller installation you saw in London, "From the Freud Museum." How did you arrive at Hiller's work? As a fictional museum it is very different to the other museums you visit in *Routes*: were you consciously trying to play off the differences between the two?

JC: I first learned about Susan Hiller in the early 1980s through the American poet, Barbara Einzig, who has since edited an important collection, *Thinking*

About Art: Conversations With Susan Hiller. It was Hiller's anthropological/archaeological background, and her incorporation of issues from those disciplines in her painting, photography, videos, and installations, that most interested me. I suppose I assimilated her to my utopian category of "ethnographic surrealism." She is deeply concerned with "cultural" grounds for ways of perceiving and feeling, for the real that's taken for granted. She has worked with dreams, as everyday forms of knowing, in ways reminiscent of Leiris in his "oneirographic" writings from *Nuits Sans Nuit* (*Nights as Day, Days as Nights*). Hiller is interested in expanded notions of writing and inscription. Her work draws— in anti-primitivist ways—on tribal and other non-Western sources. Moreover, she has been very interested in matters of taxonomy and collecting, sometimes in ways similar to what Bataille and Co. were doing in the journal *Documents*, at least as I reconstructed it. Crucially, for me, she adds a strong woman's perspective to this very masculinist tradition. I don't know whether Hiller would be happy or not to be aligned this way. There are plenty of other sources. But it's how I came to her beautiful and unsettling work.

You say my piece on Hiller is about a kind of "fictional museum." Maybe it seems so because of its fragmented, subjective voice. But I see her presence in the Freud Museum as helping transform a shrine into a "contact zone." So the stakes there are the same as in the other museums visited in *Routes*. And the chapter is actually quite documentary in all its evocations; it doesn't make anything up. I happened to be in

London and read about Hiller's installation in the newspaper. She used objects and texts arranged in archaeological collecting boxes to interrupt Freud's famous collections of Egyptian and Classical antiquities. She provided other "origins," other "sources" of meaning and "civilization." Drawing from Australian aboriginal materials, from female cults in Greece, from Joanna Southcott, from water-witching, from Mayan traditions, from African tourist art, from Sephardic Jewish history, etc. Hiller supplemented Freud's masculine, European, world view in a way that gently, firmly pried open that tradition. It was never a question of consigning Freud to the junk heap of history, but rather of placing him in a complex intersection of histories. I felt immediately at home with this project, and thought it was a model of what I had, in different ways, been trying to do with Western anthropological discourses and institutions such as the museum.

I started out just trying to describe and appreciate Hiller's intervention. But, under her spell perhaps, I became as interested in the Freud Museum itself as in her poignant collection boxes. I heard a woman's voice wafting across from another room. Anna Freud, narrating home movies about her parents—films shot by Marie Bonaparte. Freud at Burlington Gardens, dying, surrounded by women. In the present Museum, Anna's workroom rivals her father's. And her own life—with its travels, friendships, and clinical, intellectual work—pervades the space. Freud's own death here, a victim of Hitler's ethnic cleansing, writing a book, *Moses and Monotheism* that undermined race purity (Moses the Egyptian), his struggle to sustain a kind of lucidity in the gathering obscurity, and the need to find a home, a garden, in exile—all this is intensely moving. It's moving even as, indeed because, one knows that the civilizational world Freud collected and cherished was crumbling around him and would be forever altered by world war and its aftermaths. (I feel similarly about another great "end of the West" work of erudition written in exile during the war, Eric Auerbach's *Mimesis*.)

And then London itself—"postcolonial," "diasporic"—crowded into the essay, which was already faceting almost out of control. I had to find a place, somehow, for Blake's transformative vision, and for another museum, of the city of London, which was just then holding a special exhibit called "The Peopling of London" (nothing but immigrants from the Romans on). So the piece turned into a kind of intersectional meander which, I'm afraid, is formally quite precarious, but where most of my book's obsessions are going on. All the balls in the air—for the reader to catch! *Routes* makes some demands on reading. It changes voice, rhetoric, and genre from "chapter" to "chapter." Reviewers have complained about having to shift gears all the time; and of course different critics like half the pieces and hate the other half—for opposite reasons. But I thought it worth risking some confusion in order to—as my friend Jed Rasula put it—"aerate the academic text" while making explicit the different, serious registers (analytic, poetic, subjective, objective, descriptive, meditative, evocative, etc.) of thinking. We operate on many levels, waking and dreaming, as we make our way through a topic; but then we foreshorten the whole process in the service of a consistent, conclusive, voice or genre. I wanted to resist that a bit.

3. Interviewer: Manuela Ribeiro Sanches Santa Cruz, Winter 2000

MRS: Rereading your work I became quite aware of recurring themes in it, from your monograph on Maurice Leenhardt, *Person and Myth* to *Routes*: themes such as a non-static, non-essentialist concept of culture, the refusal of dichotomies, the attention to local cultures, avoiding at the same time the risk of reifying them in their difference. Your operational, descriptive concept of culture as bricolage, or as collage, seems to be already latent in *Person and Myth*.

In *Routes* you are still dealing with the tensions between the homogenizing tendencies in an ongoing globalization process and local ways of dealing with them, and you address this continuity quite explicitly, when you write that what you are proposing is "less a bounded topic than a transition from prior work—a process of translating, starting again, continuing," "prolong[ing] and continu[ing]." Do you agree with this? What has persisted, what has changed or rather been dislocated?"

JC: When I wrote the passages you quote, I had in my mind a work that has been important for me, but which has been largely forgotten: Edward Said's *Beginnings*, where he takes on the whole problem of starting up afresh, and shows that it's never possible to begin cleanly, to begin in a whole new way. One is always working with given terms, always working one's way out of certain entanglements into new entanglements. So in many ways, *Routes* is a kind of continuation, retranslation, or recontextualization of *The Predicament of Culture*. As you've said very well, there is this kind of continual worrying of the culture idea, this sense of culture as a predicament, as something that I'm stuck with, in a way, that's deeply compromised, but that I cannot quite do without. It's a bit like the Derridean idea of something under erasure, this idea of culture that I begin again with in *Routes*. One of the strands where I think I have changed or moved in a new direction is my more qualified sense of culture as an open process, and as something made or invented.

When I was writing *Routes* and *Predicament* I would be more likely to use a phrase, like the "invention of culture," or the "invention of tradition." Those are the titles of two works: one by the anthropologist Roy Wagner, the other a famous edited collection by Eric Hobsbawm and Terence Ranger. Today I would tend to use the language of articulation rather than the language of invention. I derive the notion articulation, of course, from the British cultural studies tradition and the work of Stuart Hall, reaching back originally to Gramsci. Articulation is the political connecting and disconnecting, the hooking and unhooking of elements—the sense that any socio-cultural ensemble that presents itself to us as a whole is actually a set of historical connections and disconnections. A set of elements have been combined to make a cultural body, which is also a process of disconnection, through actively sustained antagonisms. Articulations and disarticulations are constant processes in the making and remaking of cultures.

MRS: Does it then make any sense to speak of "authentic" or "inauthentic" cultures?

JC: This way of seeing things seems to me to escape the notion of inauthenticity which comes with the idea of invented or reinvented cultures and identities. And so, if one thinks of what I studied in some of my first writings on religious conversion, Melanesian peoples engaging with Christianity, one has to give up notions of before and after, leaving the old life behind and being reborn in the Christian faith and so forth. I'm inclined to rethink all that now in terms of articulation, so that in the conversion process elements of tradition get hooked onto elements of modernity and then, as modernity evolves in diverse directions including so-called postmodernity, elements of modernity can get rehooked onto elements of tradition, notions of place, new forms of indigeneity. This avoids the whole either-or, all-or-nothing, zero-sum game of cultural change in a way that, I think, is true to the messiness, the shifting power relations, the dialogical and historical open-endedness of contact-histories.

If I were to write again about the Mashpee Indians—the final chapter of *The Predicament of Culture*—I would take this perspective. And in fact I now think an articulation approach was implicit in what I did write, but at that time I didn't have the theoretical language which since then I've learned from neo-Marxian analyses of cultural process and politics.

MRS: Describing your concept of articulation, you mentioned bodies. Are there any organic elements in these bodies? I was thinking of articulation as a predominantly constructivist concept.

JC: I think we're on the same track. The word culture is deeply tied up with organic notions of growth, life, death—bodies that persist through time. All the etymologies of the word go back to cultivation. So, what articulation offers is a much more historical and political sense of the process of sustaining, making and remaking these forms. When I think of a cultural body as an articulated body, it doesn't look like an organic body. It looks more like a monster, sometimes, or perhaps a cyborg or perhaps a political alliance, a coalition in which certain elements of a population have connected with other elements, but with the possibility—which is always there in articulation—of disarticulation. There is nothing written in nature or in history that this particular group must include who it does, or be allied with that particular group. Even a time-honored kinship system will look more like a set of political alliances than something with the natural-ness of an organic body.

MRS: Could you explain in a more detailed way how the concept of culture as articulation you are now proposing may be a helpful tool to think about the changes we are facing nowadays?

JC: Articulation for me changes the way one has to think about cultural change. For example, in the Island Pacific area there is a well established way of thinking sometimes called the fatal impact story. It takes as pivotal the arrival of Western societies in Island Pacific cultures bringing their diseases, their religions, their commerce, their imperialisms, all of which have devastating and irreparable effects on local societies. The rupture is complete: fifty years later, all the people are Christians, traditional customs and languages are vanishing, etc. We know this story. We read it every week in travel accounts of remote, supposedly primitive places. The assumption is always that, because certain central elements of the culture have been destroyed, killed in effect, the culture itself must be dead. But this equates transformation, however violent, with death. It's based on the model of an organic body, in which, for example, if your lungs or heart were torn out the effect would be fatal. It's common sense...

MRS: Yes, you're right. And this is what makes people feel nostalgic about "pure" or "intact" cultures. But don't you think that there are cultures dying out? And isn't there the real danger of the corruption of beliefs, values by the ongoing process of globalization we are witnessing?

JC: What you're invoking is only half the story—an important half. But I tend to be suspicious of discourses of "corruption" because they blind us to the revival and persistence of local and indigenous movements all over the world. Many people continue to feel themselves whole and different despite the fatal impact and all the many subsequent changes. They continue to feel themselves Native Pacific Islanders, or Native Americans, or First Nations peoples of Canada. Even though they may not speak their native languages, though they may be good Christians or businessmen, these groups have built alliances linking elements of the old with the new; and while certain cultural elements have dropped away, others have been added in. So these persisting—not exactly "living"—cultures use prosthetic processes, that is, added or connecting devices more like political alliances than grafted limbs or hybrid growths. Nothing weird or bizarre, then, about Indian Gambling Casinos or Aboriginal video productions, Yup'ik Eskimo Russian

Orthodoxy or Hawaiian reggae—just the normal activity of cultures, changing and adapting in the contact zones of colonial, post-colonial and neo-colonial situations.

MRS: Your description of culture as an articulated body reminds me of Kleist's marionettes, those constructed organisms with a center of gravity in each movement, with its tension between the natural and the artificial, the organic and the mechanic. The marionette is thus not to be seen as a system, closed in itself: it opens up to differences, feeds from them without assimilating them.

JC: That's very interesting, and you're making me remember, in that Kleist story, the claim that precisely because the marionette is artificial, it has a kind of liveliness. The puppet's sense of being animated and real is intensified by the fact of its artificial non-natural quality. I've always connected that story with Roland Barthes' essay on the Bunraku puppet theatre in Japan, where you're seeing a disaggregated body, as one group of masked puppeteers is moving the limbs of the bodies with rods, and another group stands on the side, speaking, intoning the voice; so speech and body are disconnected, but then reconnected in the entire performance, where the power, the evocative power of the body, is multiplied precisely by its being visibly in pieces. That was a text that influenced me a lot, actually. That and Barthes' writings on Brecht—who is doing some of the same disaggregating around bodies, and voices, and realistic settings. I would persist in calling this a kind of realism, radically semiotic and historicist, broken free from naturalism and thus better able to grasp the complicated, uneven, patched-together continuities of contemporary cultural life.

MRS: Notwithstanding the unity I started to mention, there is a complexity in your thought and writing that makes it prone, I think, to all kinds of misunderstandings. You have been accused of being too reflexive and textual, ignoring the "real experience" of fieldwork, of de(con)structing the limits between fact and fiction, of exhibiting a too detached observing position (by Friedman), of eluding "final definitions" thus risking "inconsistency" or "ambivalence" (by Rabinow), and more recently of having too insistently stressed the "moving" element in cultures.

JC: I could obviously say a lot in a defensive mode about how I've been read by various people, but there's nothing more boring than an author insisting that he has not been read carefully enough by his critics. So I'll just pick up on a couple of things. I've been accused of a multitude of sins, many of them contradictory, as I offend in one direction and then for a different reader offend in an opposite way. I think this actually gets at an element of my own process, both of thinking and writing.

Take that word "ambivalence" you attribute to Paul Rabinow. Paul is right to point to the ambivalence in my writing. I've actually tried to turn it into a kind of lucid uncertainty, a method. I suppose another way of thinking about that might be to speak of inhabiting tensions, or antinomies, given to us by our time, by the constrains of the historical moments in which we live. We can't transcend, or step outside of, these contradictions, paradoxes, predicaments. We can, however, critically and self-consciously explore their possibilities and limits. For example, I consider the whole debate of essentialism/anti-essentialism which writers in cultural studies go round and round with, to be one such antinomy. The result can be people stuck behind their chosen barricades. My intellectual approach, for what it's worth, is not to resolve the antinomy, to search for some sort of middle space that I take to be true and rational, and then defend it systematically. I believe in dialectical interaction (but not necessarily transcendence). My method is more like tacking, as one might say in sailing. It's going out to one extreme and back across to another extreme, thus making some headway. I've always liked William Blake's aphorism: "The road of excess leads to the palace of wisdom." The goal is to see how far you can get with an approach, a metaphor, a theory, see what it opens for you, and then watch it fall apart, as everything at a certain point will fall apart, or turn into its opposite—as Blake, a great dialectician, would expect.

So, I take notions like text or writing and apply them to fieldwork and anthropology, to see what light could be shed, what productive defamiliarizing would result. And then eventually I find myself getting into trouble, discovering that the insight I am gaining from that particular term or theory had produced blindnesses in other areas. Then the challenge is to understand the process, not to dig in and defend a position, but to begin tacking in another direction where eventually the same kind of thing will occur. Now to me, for better or worse, this moving back and forth, going to excess and then going in another direction—which is never an opposite direction, of course, because when you think you're going into reverse you actually end up in a new space—is simply the movement of thought enmeshed in history. It's a process of endless repositioning, never an oscillation, always a kind of open-ended spiral of thought, a way of navigating in onrushing time.

I've tried in some respects to make that navigation visible in my work, and it's got me into trouble with those who were looking for certain kinds of consistency. They don't recognize my method of juxtaposition. To take an example from *The Predicament of Culture*: a strong textualist approach, the chapter called "On Ethnographic Authority" is placed beside "Power and Dialogue in Ethnography," on the French Africanist Marcel Griaule, in which I talk very explicitly about colonial formations of knowledge. One chapter is more formal, the other more historical; and by putting those next to each other I'm trying to set up a productive space of tension between approaches, both of which I consider necessary. Some readers simply ignore one or the other and praise or criticize me for working one side of the dialectic, while others find only inconsistency or ambivalence. As I said, I like to think there's method in the ambivalence. (But let's always keep in mind Marcel Granet's marvelous definition: "*La méthode, c'est le chemin, après qu'on l'a parcouru!*").

MRS: But these misreadings are to me the more startling as I also realize how self-reflexive, self-explanatory your texts are. I am thinking, for instance, of the role played by the introductions to your books where you provide an integrative reading of the different parts of it. How would you explain the mentioned interpretations, misreadings? How far have they been disappointing, defiant, or inspiring to your work? What have they brought you?

JC: The way some people have read my work, and that of others like me, is caught up in the current proclivity for what I call "pushing off the posts". There's a minor industry, at least in America and in Britain, of people who are establishing their own discursive identity, their own authoritative position, by saying "we are not postmoderns, not postcolonials, we are not poststructuralists." Beyond many substantial differences of analysis on questions of epistemological relativity, the coherence and future of the world system, the salience of "identity" formations, etc. (important debates that do not, in fact, line up along a single frontier), a kind of reflex rejection has developed. To some extent this polemical response is part of normal generational and institutional differentiation within intellectual life, the domain of "trends," "fads," and "back to basics" reactions. But I think it is intensified with respect to the "posts," because of a kind of general anxiety, perhaps of a millennial sort in the last couple of decades, about where in fact the world is going. I do think that the old big stories about where modernity was headed, where the West was going, today seem much less certain. What all those "posts" refer to is not some sort of rigorous historical notion about where we are. "Post" registers nothing more than the sense of a significant change, something new we don't know what to call yet. So we add "post" to some more familiar thing, drawing a line across the flow of time, a moment in which something like an emergent "period" is perceived by people who themselves are complexly and confusedly located in transition. I think that, given the breakup of a sense of teleological direction, intellectuals in the West, and unevenly in other parts of the world, "push off the posts" in the name of something more rigorous, rational, and progressively political, or something more authentic, something, in any event, less relativistic, confused, open-ended.

MRS: Maybe the intense readings and misreadings we have talked about derive also from the very diverse approaches to your work. People with quite different interests, intellectual formations, and agendas have been reacting to it —responses from anthropology, literary theory, art history, cultural studies. But I also have the impression that you are less and less preoccupied with "textual" readings, the literary critic seems to have gradually yielded to the cultural critic. The issues are very much the same, but I think you are less concerned with rhetorical strategies, discourse analysis. You still derive much of your reflection from ethnographies, but I have the impression that the discursive and political practices "outside" (to put it in a sort of reductive way) the actual ethnographies have gained more relevance. What has changed after *Writing Culture* in the world, in academia, that would explain such a shift?

JC: Well, my work has always moved between the perspectives of literary studies, history and cultural anthropology, and partly as a result of that, I find myself often addressing different audiences, with different expectations. I often function as a kind of import-export specialist between the disciplines. Looked at most cynically, the import-export person in the disciplines takes some idea that's outmoded in one field and moves it into another field, where it becomes an exciting new thing. A bit like the smuggler, the value of whose merchandise depends on the border it transgresses. More positively, I would say that the movement of ideas from one field into another field is never simply a matter of transporting an object from here to there, but is always really a matter of transla-tion. And through the process of translation in the new context what's brought across is made new; it takes on unexpected dimensions. I came to profes-sional maturity in a moment of the American academy when literary theory had an enormous prestige. It carried the epistemological authority of people like Barthes and Derrida, and it was getting applied in a lot of extra-literary domains. (I had colleagues in the '70s who complained of "literary critical imperi-alism!")

I was among those who brought literary theory to bear rather intensely on anthropological writing, especially the various forms of realist writing associated with ethnography, cross-cultural description. At the same time we were involved in expanding what could be called the ethnographic style to a wide range of contexts and methods for describing, analyzing and evoking cultural phenomena. And, since we had decoupled ethnography from anthropology, ethnography could no longer be restricted to what anthropologists did when they did proper fieldwork. Ethnography turned out to be something that could apply to all sorts of different people interpreting themselves and their communities in "cultural" terms. The notion of ethnography became rather promiscuous. People started finding out that they'd been like the *bourgeois gentilhomme* speaking prose all along: they found out they had always been doing ethnography, as insiders/outsiders in their everyday life, and so there was a kind of drastic expansion of "ethnographic" work.

One of the sites into which it expanded was literature and literary studies, but it also moved into film, media studies, museum work, a whole range of fields. Many artists, conceptual artists and otherwise, started doing explicitly ethnographic kinds of installations and analysis. The work of Fred Wilson, Rene Green, Lothar Baumgarten, people like that. So this was a fertile, somewhat anarchic period of crossovers among the fields, among the disciplines, that I associate with the '70s and the early '80s in the United States. It also involved a coalescence of many of these trends under the name "Cultural Studies," a rather different formation from the tradition of British cultural studies: the Birmingham School's heyday of the '70s and then its movement into London and the polytechnic universities during the '80s. In the United States the influence of literary studies, in more or less poststructuralist veins, predominated, to the detriment of cultural studies' updated Gramscian Marxism. The interface with anthropology, something strangely absent in Britain until recently, was strong, but conducted largely through the expanded "ethnographic" domain. For a time, virtually everything was ethnographic, to a point where the term stopped meaning anything. And there was also a tendency to turn everything into a text, with the result that all sorts of institutional, and material, economic realities got obscured.

Since the mid '80s we've seen a process of retrenching and revisionism, a process of recognizing the blindness that came with the insight. My own work has certainly moved in a kind of uneven zigzag since then. It's not that I think that those movements were useless or that they were distortions; every theory, every interpretative perspective is an intensification that distorts. The question is whether we have begun to get a perspective on the nature of the foreshortening, and may be able to learn not only from what the approach showed us, but also from what it didn't show.

MRS: In Europe we tend to think of American campuses as worlds outside the world, ivory towers.

Santa Cruz is often quoted as an example. I would also like to add that, as a visiting scholar there, I was quite surprised by the political engagement in the Center for Cultural Studies. I had the feeling that people were addressing some very important issues, while in Europe, or at least in Portugal, there seems to be an ongoing tendency to the non-political. It is difficult to generalize. On the other hand in Portugal there are discussions about the humanities becoming more competitive. Curricula should be changed in order to attract more students. Some people fear that cultural studies with its interest for media or youth cultures may be co-opted and neutralized, others that it may usurp the terrain of literary studies. Others again react to postcolonial or diasporic studies seeing in them the danger of the dissolution of the canon or a menace to "national integrity"—some Europeans even go so far as to consider "identity politics" and its influence outside the U.S. academy as mere "American cultural imperialism." This to contextualize the discussion. How different is your experience? I guess working in the UCSC History of Consciousness Program is a very special situation. And what about the relations between anthropology and cultural studies?

JC: In the U.S. context— at least where I work—the '70s and the '80s saw rather dramatic interdisciplinary work in many fields, particularly in the humanities and the interpretative social sciences. But now we are, as I've said, in a period of disciplinary reformation. We find literary theorists saying, for example, wait a minute, we're not just cultural-studies ethnographers.

There's something to literary analysis that has its own specificity. I see a reconnection with tradition in many fields. But it's not—even though sometimes it is portrayed that way—a reactionary, "back to basics," movement. There is no going back. I see a rearticulation, a reformation of the domain of the "literary" in response to the border crossings that have occurred, and that are still going on. Similarly, we can see a renegotiation of borders around anthropology, as it draws lines with respect to "textualism," as it distinguishes itself from "cultural studies." Many want to rethink and reclaim what is specifically anthropological about their disciplinary kind of ethnography— "fieldwork." Or, if anthropology has a distinctive use of the "culture" idea, what is that distinctive idea? Is there anything left of the notion of Man—capital M—which once united the various sub-disciplines of anthropology? I don't think there's anything left myself, but there's plenty of debate about that today.

I see this as the normal process of what I would call disciplining, which is something I write about in *Routes*, a process of working borders. Borders are never walls that can't be crossed, borders are always lines selectively crossed: there's a simultaneous management of borders and a process of subversion. There are always smugglers, as well as border police. And often the smugglers and the border police depend on each other for their jobs, for the value of what they do. But the permeability, the crossings of borders, needs to be renegotiated periodically, and I think that is certainly going on now. A lot of extra-anthropological stuff was taken into the discipline, from literature, from history, from feminism and from cultural studies. And a lot of "cultural" stuff has entered literature and the rest from anthropology. This is all to the good, I think. But then as those intellectual communities begin to lose their sense of identity, of their core tradition, then an aggressive rearticulation of insides and outsides takes place. The current reaction can't last forever, to be sure, since any discipline that builds impregnable walls around itself, like any society, is dooming itself to a kind of museum life.

All knowledge is interdisciplinary; knowledge does not naturally fall into disciplinary forms. At the same time, disciplines, like tools, are useful, because you can't explain everything at once. You can't master all methodologies at the same time, and mastery requires specialization. There are good reasons for disciplines, but they need to be seen as historically in motion and relational. I've had the unusual academic fate of being positioned between fields. I was trained in history, always liked literature as much or more than history and had a deepening fascination with anthropology. I've been fortunate enough to work for more than two decades in a program that has wanted me precisely to juggle the three balls of history, literature and anthropology.

MRS: Does this mean that working in the History of Consciousness Program has had a decisive influence on your work, or would you say that your interests would have led you anyway to the path you have taken?

JC: The interests were there, but I'm realistic enough about the disciplinary force of communities to know that if my first job had been in a History Department I would not have written anything like what I in fact wrote. So I feel fortunate to have been in a program where there was permission to cross-over, to mix and match. I had colleagues, particularly Hayden White, Norman O. Brown, and Donna Haraway, who encouraged and inspired me to do just this. So I'm a bit of a special case. But I would hasten to say that the kind of work I've done has been successfully pursued within disciplines by people working the edges of their own communities. It doesn't require utopian spaces like the History of Consciousness Program. It's actually, as I've already suggested, part of the interdisciplinary process of disciplining, a necessary feature of knowledge which waxes and wanes in the social life of ideas. I've spoken a bit about the expanding and contracting of interdisciplinarity over the last twenty-five years or so in the U.S. But the tempo of these processes varies in different contexts, and what's happening in Europe, Mexico, or Australia may be quite different.

MRS: Although very sympathetic to indigenous causes, faced with discussions on concrete examples of indigenous claims, I have almost suspected you were becoming an essentialist. My fear of essentialisms results from European experiences, such as destructive nationalisms and ethnicisms: Nazi Germany and its celebration of "blood and soil," Sarajevo and Kosovo, not to speak of a very narrow concept of Portuguese identity cultivated by the dictatorship with its emphasis on tradition and continuity, and significantly associated with the ideology of colonial "universalism." I am more and more aware how much I too am prey to other forms of localism, as you may be able to derive from my obviously Eurocentric associations.

JC: I suppose, with regard to that question of essentialism and anti-essentialism, I am in tune with writers like Paul Gilroy, in *The Black Atlantic*, trying to articulate an anti-anti-essentialist position. The two negatives do not, of course, add up to a positive, and so the anti-anti-essentialist position is not a simple return to essentialism. It recognizes that a rigorously anti-essentialist attitude, with respect to things like identity, culture, tradition, gender, socio-cultural forms of that kind, is not really a position one can sustain in a consistent way. One can't communicate at all without certain forms of essentialism (assumed universals, linguistic rules and definitions, typifications and even stereotypes). Certainly one can't sustain a social movement or a community without certain apparently stable criteria for distinguishing us from them. These may be, as I've said before, articulated in connections and disconnections, but, as they are expressed and become meaningful to people, they establish accepted truths. Certain key symbols come to define the we against the they; certain core elements of a tradition come to be separated out, venerated, fetishized, defended. This is the normal process, the politics, by which groups form themselves into identities and people recognize each other within a set of symbols

and conventions. They do this for better and for
worse, and we need to be able to distinguish the
"essentialism" of, say, the East Timorese resisting
Indonesian annexation in the name of their peoplehood from Milošević's Serbian chauvinism.
Epistemology isn't very helpful here. We need historical specificity and an analysis of social inequality and
power. Now, we might in a kind of abstract, purely
philosophical way find that all these political and
cultural machinations are somehow done in bad faith.
But of course just because cultural essentialism has
been theoretically refuted doesn't make it go away.

MRS: But I found it difficult to understand your
apparently too quick empathy with certain issues in
indigenous movements, like biologically grounded
land claims, or Hawaiian hereditary monarchy and the
stress of blood ties.

This is one of the reasons why when I was in
Santa Cruz universals seemed again important to me.
Of course I realize the limits and unsustainability of
such abstract essentialisms, even when we admit they
are not a mere expression or a strategy of Western
hegemony. But I am still suspicious of identity politics
as practiced in the United States: don't they divide too
much?

JC: I don't think we will get beyond so-called identity
politics. And when I contemplate the project of
sustaining a rigorous anti-essentialism I sometimes
think of the Futurists coming to Paris before World
War One—do you recall the photos, all of them

buttoned up in dark suits?—decreeing that representations of the nude should be banned for fifty years! Prescriptive anti-essentialisms are a bit like that. The point really is to develop a critical notion of the various forms of essentialism, when, and where, and how they are deployed. It's just a bad utopianism, and rather condescending, to think that claims to roots, tradition, identity, and purportedly natural attachments should be opposed across the board. This is something that has been rudely impressed on the theoretical sophisticates of my own generation. For just at the moment all the radical post-structuralisms became popular in the U.S. academy a whole range of formerly marginal and excluded peoples and perspectives were fighting for recognition: women, racial and ethnic minorities, new immigrants. These groups, for the first time entering this public sphere, often felt the sophisticated cultural critics to be, in effect, telling them "Oh yes, we understand your gender, race, culture and identity are important to you, but you know, you're just essentializing." Well, the insurgents were not amused, and some bitter polemics around theory and the potentially reactionary effects of rigid anti-essentialisms were a part of the transformations, the struggles, the wars around authority and cultural identity, which have been a fundamental part of life in the post-'60s U.S. academy.

In that context, finding ways to take "identity politics" seriously, while also sustaining the possibility of outside critical perspectives with respect to the claims and symbols of these movements is a difficult—but, I think, extremely important—struggle that various of us have tried to maintain, with uneven success. We have found support from insurgent scholars and activists who, from their own perspective, are critics of essentialism, but often in a non-absolute, historically contingent, dialogically and politically engaged way. The current moment is one of contin- uous struggle around essentialist claims both within and outside the various identity struggles. And in that sense the '60s rigueur are inescapable elements of the scene. Perhaps from your perspective my own thinking flirts too closely with essentialisms of one sort or another. I find I need to do that in order to stay engaged with the concrete situation I'm in, and not to seek some place of philosophical or political purity which would evade the historical conjuncture and its cultural politics.

MRS: In that sense I think your way of thinking about culture as articulation is very helpful, as it offers a more complex way to deal with such issues. On the other hand I am reminded of one of your Jardin des Plantes postcards. There you speak of *le vertige hori- zontal,* "one of those miracles of travel," of "trans- planted civilization" and, quoting Alicia Dujovne Ortiz: "But if I have no roots, why have my roots hurt me so." And you get "infatuated" with the palms of the Luxembourg gardens "symmetrical, perfect in boxes with iron feet. Vegetable extraterrestrials." I recently visited the Berlin Jewish Museum by Daniel Liebeskind. What impressed me was the way the building proposes an articulation between Jewish culture and the city and how the tension between past and present, light and darkness, and the refusal of right angles and classical symmetry leads us to consider not only the suffering of exile and holocaust, but also the utopian moments of redemption, as suggested in the "Garden of Exile" or the "E. T. A. Hoffman Garden" by the olive trees planted on top of concrete pillars, aerial but rooted, like the palm trees in the Jardin des Plantes.

JC: Yes, and what's powerful, too, is the way the concrete pillars are leaning, as if blown by that Benjaminian wind of history. I'm glad you picked up on my little image from the Jardin des Plantes in *The Predicament of Culture*: palm trees in the Luxemburg gardens, wonderfully, perfectly rooted, but in boxes which hover a few inches off the ground and are held up by wrought-iron feet. I guess this is the kind of "rooting" that appeals to me! One wouldn't want to say those palms really aren't rooted at all. But the roots hover a bit; they are on legs. I'm interested in all the roots that are on wheels or carried by jumbo jet airplanes these days. Kwame Anthony Appiah, himself complexly attached to Ghana, Britain and the United States, recently wrote in a memoir of his Ghanaian father about taking your roots with you. I find it good to think with that kind of paradoxical mobile rooted-ness, because in practice people are living all sorts of tactical combinations of roots and routes, experiences too easily mapped onto oppositions of stasis and displacement, essence and difference, native and cosmopolitan...

MRS: I like your tactical "tacking" and the way you move back and forth between what sometimes seems to me Hegelian dialectics and a very nominalist, pragmatic, ethnographically sustained approach. A nominalist and a cynic who believes in the redemptive moment of small utopias, or in the Messiah, as you once told me, after a discussion on the limits of stoic universals.

I must also confess that, faced with the conference held at Santa Cruz in February, 2000, "Native Pacific Cultural Studies on the Edge," I had to reconsider my anti-essentialist, anti-nationalist rigueur, and my newly rediscovered preference for detached stoic-like universal rationales. It was for me a very strange feeling to hear indigenous Pacific scholars speaking about their culture, their need to find new theories and epistemologies, that might enable them to build their own cultural studies area. And in the process they were invoking things EurAms would hardly venture to speak about on such an occasion, such as long term friendships and other personal complicities, using affective ties to reinforce institutional and political alliances. These were not projected "natives," as in some travel accounts I had read, but full subjects on their own terms, fighting for a discipline not only as a pure theoretical, academic matter, but as something intrinsically political. The native Pacific was claiming a complexly traditional and postmodern existence. The fact is that my Euro-scepticism regarding essentialisms, nationalisms, ethnicisms was somehow tempered by this very warm and very rainy weekend in sunny California. And scepticism, moderated by a restrained utopian enthusiasm, may also be a good way of "tacking," sailing against the wind. As the history goes, Portuguese were for a while experts in the art of tacking...

I have mentioned your "Postcards from Paris." Besides this text, "White Ethnicity," "Immigrant," and "Fort Ross Meditation" (all in *Routes*) are what I would call examples of a more openly "experimental," "literary," "subjective" writing. What you call "personal explorations" seem to me to comment on your more "academic" texts. How do these two types of discourse relate to each other? Do they fit together? And then there are people who prefer your more scholarly writing in *Person and Myth*, although I must say it can be quite unorthodox too.

JC: You ask about the different styles and modes of writing that I use, and my sense of what the relation is between the literary and the scholarly, the poetic and the prosaic, etc. And you suggest that some people prefer my more scholarly writing in *Person and Myth*. Well, in that biography the writing isn't uniformly conventional—there are a few, we might say, experimental turns—but there is a continuous object, a life, and a more or less continuous, descriptive, analytic/evocative tone sustained throughout. No doubt this makes it more acceptable to some readers. While I do try to problematize the idea of a continuous life and of a biography, I don't do it in the form of the book itself for tactical reasons that I explain in my introduction.

But since then I've allowed myself to experiment with more than one style within the covers of a single book. I'm self-consciously pushing against the law of genre—that contract between reader and audience which determines the mode of reception, the rhetoric, the rules of evidence and argument and so forth—within particular forms of writing. And to be quite honest, I'm not sure ultimately just why I do this. It's not that I think "scholarly genres" are restrictive and must be transgressed, or that "poetic" evocation is liberating. But perhaps I'm not unique in finding that my process of "thinking through" a topic—whether it is the problematic of culture, in *The Predicament of Culture*, whether it's contemporary travel and displacement in the sequel *Routes*—takes place in a number of registers. Some of these are scholarly and analytical, some of them evocative or poetic.

And I think that, at least for me, whatever sense of complexity and richness I can derive in the hermeneutic process, has to do with crossing among these several registers. Don't we all operate on more than one level of consciousness and desire? Gaston Bachelard wrote somewhere that you can't really know a topic until you've dreamed it. And wasn't it Apollinaire who put a sign outside his door, when he was sleeping during the day: *Le poète travaille*? And why not the sleeping scholar, the scholar at work: *Le savant travaille*? I've wanted to open up a bit the range of processes that go into what we consider to be thought, and even methodical research: some of it very orderly and disciplined, some of it much more

free-flowing and open-ended, and in a sense meditative. I like the notion of meditation, a more inclusive
word for the real range of processes involved. But why
is it that when we come to write about what we've
been thinking, meditating, dreaming, researching, we
have to foreshorten a multifarious process into a single
rhetoric, one overarching form?

For better or worse, I've always found that
focus to be constraining. So I've tended to write in a
number of styles and to produce books that look like
collages or juxtapositions of genres. My goal hasn't
been to blend the different styles, not to say that academic writing really should be poetry or anything like
that. It's not about blurring, it's about juxtaposing, and
thus making people conscious of the rules of engagement, as it were, determining their reception. So I
make demands on my readers, I ask them to shift
gears. I was doing some of that in *The Predicament of
Culture* and I've done rather more in *Routes*. Some of
the book's "chapters" really look a lot like poems;
some are travel accounts; one is an evocative little
book review; and a number are rather developed
scholarly arguments with lots of footnotes and so
forth. The final chapter, "Fort Ross Meditation," is
written in a rather personal scholarly voice—trying to
exemplify the form of the meditation for serious
historical-cultural analysis. So as the book's readers
turn to each new chapter, they have to rather quickly
get a take, a read, on what sort of a form is coming at
them. Some readers feel that this isn't quite fair and
they work to separate the wheat from the chaff. One
reviewer of *Routes* will like half of the pieces and

dislike the other half, and then another reviewer will have exactly the opposite reaction. That may be inevitable, given the diversity of styles and forms in that book. Of course, there's plenty of room for criticism of these experiments, and I'm the last to know how successful I've been.

MRS: In the Prologue to *Routes* you describe it very self-reflexively as a "collage," as "paths and not a map," "bring[ing] parts together while sustaining a tension between them." (This reminds me very much of Benjamin's concept of constellation.) Your models are modernists and surrealists but your work has been labeled postmodern. I am aware of hesitations concerning the modernism and postmodernism in your work. You describe yourself ironically as "a sometime postmodern (liking) contamination;" and there is a direct grappling with the issue in "Paradise" when you ask if your "concern and (taste) for cultural/historic juxtapositions [is] part of an 'englobing appetite,' a 'hegemonic,' 'postmodern irony,'" and whether your work really helped establish a new "intellectual imperialism." Going back to the surrealists. You mention that your interest in "cultural collage and incongruity derives quite explicitly from modernist art and poetry: the Cubists, Dada and international Surrealism, Segalen, Conrad, Leiris, Williams, and Césaire," all of whom figure prominently in *The Predicament of Culture*.

JC: I have never been comfortable with the label postmodern, or postmodernist, as attached to my work, and I think if people read *The Predicament of Culture* they'll see that I almost never use the term. On the other hand, since so many have insisted on calling me a postmodernist, I have to accept that there must be something to it. But my own view is that the line between postmodernist and modernist is always going to be fuzzy and debatable. I said before that the very notion of "post" can never adequately describe some whole new perspective or epoch but merely a sense of change or something "after," still entangled in what we know and can name. I certainly think of my writing as caught up with and empowered by modernism. You mentioned the surrealists, Conrad, Leiris, Williams, Césaire, people like that; and that's certainly the way I would locate myself.

Now taking a figure like William Carlos Williams, one could produce a reading that would make him a postmodernist *avant la lettre*. And there may be a sense in which my use of him, my updating, does something like that. He's of course a different kind of modernist, unlike the canonical figures Joyce, Picasso, etc., who are very much associated with the great Western centers, such as New York or Paris. Williams is more decentered. He makes a self-conscious move to the local—a local that is not outside of connection with the larger circuits of power, of literary and cultural influence, but which is a kind of strategic marginalization. I'm referring, of course, to Williams' famous choice to locate himself in New Jersey, not far from New York to be sure, but definitely in a small town, adopting there the specific, quasi-ethnographic, standpoint of a family doctor.

And this was a time when doctors went into people's houses, so he derives an acute sense of a localism—of accent, of body types, of ethnicities—in the immigrant, working-class communities of New Jersey. Now, there's something for me very attractive about adopting that engaged, hands-on, perspective. So Williams is perhaps someone who prefigures an expansive vision of the "ethnographic," a vision located not primarily in London, Paris, New York, Vienna, Berlin, where modernist culture was elaborated, but which interests itself in out-of-the-way places.

When I speak like that, it starts to sound like the language of certain "postmodernisms." But it's important to say that Williams is not a nomad, is not displaced in that normative poststructuralist sense which sometimes turns the observation that people are multiply positioned and displaced in the contemporary world into a prescription that they should be multiply positioned and displaced. Williams understood the fact of multiple location and positioning and consciously chose to localize himself. I suppose he is analogous to those palms in their boxes: He sinks roots, he localizes himself, strategically. Rutherford, New Jersey is not the place he was born; he has a very complex multinational familial background. Williams puts down artificial roots, but in a lifelong way, tied to an engaged practice and involvement with neighborhoods, people, their bodies. This simultaneously intimate and analytic medical practice produces a set of writings which go well beyond poetry, narrowly defined.

And, once again, this is not some sort of definitive return to the local. I see it as the construction of a local/global place. While Williams writes his epic *Paterson* from the standpoint of a fading industrial city, he stays in contact with the most "advanced" art and literary scene in New York. And he knows quite well what's happening in Paris. These high modernist places are simply parts of his world, not its center. It's that sense of off-centered connectedness that I have found so interesting, in my foreshortened reading from the late twentieth century. The exercise may, at least, give a sense of the sort of anachronistic, apro-gressive postmodernist I am—if I am a postmodernist.

MRS: You have mentioned "Identity in Mashpee" and the importance of that trial for your further thinking. Could you elaborate?

JC: Well, the essay about the Mashpee trial has played a central role in the development of my thinking. In a Boston federal court in 1978 a group of Indians on Cape Cod had to prove that they were a tribe in order to have status to sue for land. I sat in on this trial, more or less by chance, and became engrossed. I saw all the concepts I had been studying historically—the notions of culture, of history and of historical continuity, identity and so forth—efficiently torn apart by lawyers. And I saw a very complicated and apparently discontinuous history of Native American peoples in New England being put together and pulled apart by the various discourses in the courtroom. I attended the proceedings and kept extensive notes. I actually gave a talk based on the trial very soon afterwards, and then I put it aside for seven years or so, unsure I really had the authority, as a mere observer in the courtroom, to write about this history. But I eventually decided I could write it up, since it would appear at the end of my book *The Predicament of Culture*, and would be obviously tied in with all the themes in the book.

I hoped it would be evident that I was not giving a definitive or complete picture of the trial or the history of the Indian peoples in Mashpee or New England, but that I was in fact reading this event through my own obsessions, my own interests. People have, of course, criticized me for giving definitive versions of Mashpee and the trial, even though in the essay I finally wrote I tried to position myself carefully in the observer's seat of the courtroom. I didn't, in other words, try to adopt a position either of omni-science or of mobile authority. I tried to maintain a clear, partial perspective. In retrospect I see that I was using the very difficult and in many ways still enig-matic history revealed and obscured at the trial. I was using this paradigm, if you like, as a kind of transition in my own work.

The trial pushed me beyond my early focus on the history of European anthropology and exoticism, with a particular emphasis on textual forms of critique. And it led me into a concern with the possibilities and limits of indigenous agency, dynamism, and self-repre-sentation. The next thing that I wrote after the Mashpee text, an essay republished in *Routes*, was an account of "Four Northwest Coast Museums," two of which were tribal museums/cultural centers. There I was preoccupied with the processes by which indigenous communities on Vancouver Island in Canada—Kwagiulth (or Kwakwaka'wakw, formerly Kwakiutl)—reappropriated the institution of the museum. Founding museums was a condition for the repatriation of artifacts from the national collections in Canada. In the process the native communities transformed a dominant Western institution for the purposes of telling an anti-colonial tribal history. They also combined the functions of display and use, for cultural outsiders and insiders. This resourcefulness recalled the complex way the Mashpee had survived over several centuries of brutal war and intense pressures to acculturate in New England. I saw how foreign institutions such as the tribe, or the museum, externally imposed institutions, were being made and remade, translated for indigenous use. And that theme became a dominant issue in my thinking. So in some ways I'm still trying to figure out the Mashpee case, the improbable, possible persistence of Native peoples in New England. The very complex processes of tribal continuity, in colonial situations of great violence and relentless pressure, have preoccupied me. And I've come to think that the contemporary emergence of indigenous politics and contestations into new and larger, articulated public spheres is one of the really important developments of the late twentieth century.

MRS: This reminds me of the importance of thinking about the local in ways that may pay due attention to the ongoing changes in our contemporary interconnected world. How can a transnational critical cultural studies articulate the local and the global? How can we think of ways of surpassing, while maintaining, our local ways of speaking, writing, teaching, developing at the same time ways of communicating and research strategies that may allow smaller communities/countries to participate more adequately and visibly in the "global discussion"? In Portugal, where we are very much aware of such dependencies and possibilities, we are, I think, very interested in such strategies.

JC: That's a very large set of issues. I've been focusing on what I call articulated sites of indigeneity, particularly in the Pacific—returning in some of my recent work to the Southwest Pacific, Melanesia, where my first book was centered. I see this as working toward a historically rich, non-reductive account of transnational cultural politics. The strand of analysis I'm extending developed through a critique of notions of "ideology" in late capitalist situations, a critique stemming from the moment of the New Left in Britain. After 1960 people like Raymond Williams, E. P. Thompson, and Stuart Hall grappled with the fact that the old economistic models and trade union politics were simply not dealing with facts like the Americanization of Britain, new patterns of consumption, religion, youth cultures, race and gender, a whole range of things that couldn't be rounded up in an older class-based view of the political.

The best cultural studies work demonstrated the relative autonomy of cultural politics from economic determinations, while not severing the links and allowing "culture" to be reified and float free. By rejecting economic determinism it opened a breach in modernizing, Euro-centered teleologies. But it was still very much centered in Britain, in a small range of "advanced" capitalist situations. In the past couple of decades, however, we have seen the emergence of "diasporic" theories, Subaltern Studies, the recognition of Caribbean and South Asian histories and spaces within Britain, and the traveling of cultural studies itself into places like Australia, New Zealand and the U.S. We are starting to see the cultural politics of late capitalism, articulated with local places and histories all over the globe, analyzed in ways which avoid economistic reductions and top-down, system-centered visions of the planet. The challenge is to see the world whole—or whole enough—while leaving room for the kinds of dialectical and ambivalent histories I've been trying to articulate in this interview.

4. Interviewer: Robert Borofsky
Honolulu/Santa Cruz, Winter 2000

RB: Can you explain the intellectual trajectory that brought you into the Pacific? You have mentioned that it was almost by accident that you became interested in the region.

JC: Initially, I had no intention of studying anything connected with the Pacific. But then I stumbled on Maurice Leenhardt. Writing about his life plunged me into the history of French colonial New Caledonia. I encountered a brutal colonial history and, at the same time, a remarkable history of cultural survival and transformation. Kanaks, the island's Melanesian inhab-

itants, were said to be dying out. Yet they have
persisted. One of the ways they survived was by
becoming Christian, and religious conversion turned
out to be a complex process, as Leenhardt put it, of
"acculturation in two directions." Melanesian
Christianity would be a different, a new kind, of
Christianity—a way of making the best of a bad situation and a strategy for continuing to be Kanak in a
new context. I had to understand a concatenation of
elements, both very old and very new, in an original,
fraught cultural and political experience.

It all seemed very contemporary, somehow,
and I found myself wanting to think of Melanesia as
the future, not as the past. The experience broke
down historical categories, in my North-Atlantic
mind. Recognizing the Kanaks' resourcefulness and
ability to work with innovation, I gained a better sense
of interactive process, an understanding enhanced by
reading Roy Wagner who, at the time (1975), was
writing about the invention of culture in Papua New
Guinea. What I had to grasp in New Caledonia was
the politics of culture in an unequal colonial situation.
While I developed and applied this processual
perspective in other contexts later on, this is really
where I first grappled with it.

After this encounter with a Melanesian history,
I passed through poststructuralist critiques of ethnographic writing to post-colonial theory and cultural
studies. The writing of Raymond Williams and E. P.
Thompson had been crucial to me in graduate school,
and I was able to build on that, in transnational
contexts, through the work of Stuart Hall, Paul

Gilroy, Hazel Carby, Kobena Mercer, Avtar Brah and many others. The evolving British tradition of cultural studies, with its concern for post-colonial relations and for complex historical formations of "identity," seemed another version, differently mapped, of what I saw in Melanesia.

The theorizing of Stuart Hall, for example, offered tools that would have helped me with the interactive self-fashioning of Leenhardt and his converts. And Hall's neo-Gramscian approach to cultural politics has guided my continuing interest in rearticulations of tradition and the emergence of new coalitions of indigenous identity, processes very active in the Pacific. But I've always had the sense that "Pacific Cultural Studies," should such a thing take shape, would have to be different in important ways from the North-Atlantic varieties.

RB: Despite your own enthusiasm for the Pacific, the region rarely seems to attract the same amount of intellectual attention as do various other areas of the globe. What do you think accounts for the region's intellectual isolation?

JC: It's something that puzzles me and has puzzled me for some time. In Euro-American contexts of intellectual work, I try to interject Pacific examples that I think will be particularly provocative. But people often seem to glaze over. I'm something of a booster for the Western Pacific—a deeply complex and fascinating part of the contemporary world, a mind boggling place. Take, for example, the fact that the island of

New Guinea—Papua New Guinea and Irian Jaya/West Papua—contains, by some counts, 20% of the world's languages. Once one digests this astonishing news, it makes an emerging "nation" like Papua New Guinea something extremely interesting to imagine!

Sometimes I think of New Guinea as almost archetypically postmodern. Its not just a backward place catching up, traveling "from the Stone Age to the Modern World in a few generations," as popular common sense has it. The region's overlaid temporalities can't be captured by familiar evolutionist or developmentalist projections. Its cultural dynamics are contemporary in a peculiarly hybrid and broken, yet connected, way that's increasingly characteristic of cultural conglomerations. In my mind, places like Papua New Guinea and Vanuatu are exemplary contexts for thinking about the articulated sites of an unfinished modernity—fractured, sutured, overlaid, incredibly diverse, yet hooked up, complexes of local, national, regional, and global elements.

One can, of course, find plenty of places in the world to grapple with such complexities. But for me, thinking from Euro-North America, the Pacific has a special clarity. Because its places have been so firmly held in a primitivist space/time warp—"back then" and "out there"—they have never been perceived as modern. This persistent exoticism may be a blessing in disguise, once we break with the romanticism and condescension that long accompanied it. When we try to conceptualize the contemporary Pacific we may be less oriented by all the familiar modernist and modernizing narratives, and perhaps we can see how Pacific

Island places never really fit those projections. This makes it easier to imagine what might be called "aprogressive narratives of modernity," something both empirically and politically important to do.

Pacific societies participate in the contemporary world less encumbered by the assumptions that came with the modernist visions either of liberal capitalism or anti-imperialist national liberation. Seen as a complex, dynamic region, the ex-primitive, neo-traditional, para-postmodern Island Pacific confounds teleologies. And for me, at least, that makes it very good to think with.

RB: One of the ways the Pacific remains distinctive is in how it embraced decolonization, or perhaps more precisely phrased, how decolonization embraced it. It involved a more complex, ambiguous set of processes than occurred say in Africa or Asia.

JC: The timing of decolonization in the Pacific seems crucial to me. Changes in political sovereignty mostly came in the 1970s and the1980s—a couple of decades after the classical experiences of African or South Asian independence. Occurring later, decolonization in the Pacific took place—is still taking place—in a different historical context. For one thing, the notion that political independence under the leadership of nationalizing elites will lead to liberation and social justice, particularly for indigenous peoples, has been pretty definitively exploded in many parts of the world. Nation-state affiliations no longer seem, so unambiguously, the royal road to a better future.

And secondly, the capitalist world system has been going through some important mutations, beginning in the early 1970s and emerging as what's variously called flexible accumulation, late capitalism, post-Fordism, or post-modernity. As a result, the very idea, the rallying cry, of independence seems increasingly to have quotation marks placed around it. The notion of sovereignty, that sense of control over borders, over culture, over economy, is complicated by the fact that no nation, not even the most powerful, now has control over its economy and over its cultural symbols. The same holds true for borders: The movement of populations is dramatic and often non-linear. Experiences of citizenship and identity are often complexly divided between places. One can be born and live in California, for instance, and still be strongly connected to Hawai'i, to Samoa, to Tonga.

Of course, such dynamics existed previously. But their salience for cultural, for trans-cultural, politics was not at all clear in the 1950s and '60s. A modernist vision of nationhood held sway, a vision of drawing lines around particular territories and building imagined communities inside. Nation-building—making "Nigerians" or "Indonesians," for example—in ethnically-complex territories, involved reducing or opposing retrograde "tribalisms." The nation alone could be progressive.

Such ideas are, of course, far from dead. But things are inescapably ambiguous today. Pulling against such attitudes are revived projects of the indigenous and the local. These developments reflect traditional regional differences, new "ethnic" antagonisms, as well as the pressures and opportunities of a capitalist world system that, as Jonathan Friedman has argued, actively makes room for, and to a degree commodifies, the politics of localism, identity, and culture. I would insist, however, on the phrase "to a degree," as I think Friedman and many historically-minded ethnographers of the Pacific would too. The sources and outcomes of the cultural and political articulations often reductively termed "identity politics" are historically complex and locally, regionally dynamic.

In the context, then, of "belated" Pacific decolonization—or what I like to call post-/neo-colonialism—the forms of political sovereignty being hammered out take all kinds of forms. Stuart Firth's essay in your collection *Remembrance of Pacifics Past* is a good opening. Because decolonization comes to the Pacific when sovereignty is an increasingly ambiguous and contested concept, we are seeing the emergence of different forms of national identity, new sorts of negotiations among the local, the regional, the national, and the global. In this light, it might be illuminating to compare questions of regionalism and sovereignty in the Pacific with the same issues in the European Union—without recourse to notions of margin and center, backward and advanced.

RB: One of the Pacific's interesting aspects is its "Sea of Islands" to use Epeli Hau'ofa's phrase. What is your impression regarding this multiplex, overlapping, interactive sense of "islands" as a way of conceptualizing identity?

JC: I am very taken with Hau'ofa's struggle to get Islanders to see themselves and the spaces between them not as dots in a vast ocean but as a sea of islands which they themselves create through old and new practices of travel, visiting, trade, and migration. I am struck by the way he is able to connect old stories and modern situations, recognizing temporal overlays in a complexly con-temporary space. Hau'ofa's sea of islands is not the "Pacific Rim," of course, a regional-ization based on capital flows, with an empty center. It's a region cobbled together from the inside out, based on everyday practices, and linking islands with each other and with mainland diasporas. Hau'ofa is reaching back to voyaging canoes and, at the same time, telling stories about jumbo jets. Tongans, Samoans, and Hawaiians, for example, going back and forth to Los Angeles and Las Vegas. Like Paul Gilroy's "Black Atlantic," or emerging connections across the indigenous "Arctic," the Pacific "sea of islands" helps us conceptualize practices of subaltern region-making, realities invisible to more top-down, center-periphery, models of globalization and locality.

Such Pacific mobilities map, with unmistakable clarity, a kind of indigenous cosmopolitanism. Yet there's a paradox, a rich tension, here. Hau'ofa's later essay (in *Remembrance of Pacifics Past*) on habitat and memory brings it out clearly, I think. To recognize a specifically indigenous dialectic of dwelling and trav-eling requires more than simply unmaking the exoti-cist/colonialist concept of the homebody native, always firmly in place. I've learned a lot from Island-savvy students at Santa Cruz—Vince Diaz, Teresia

Teaiwa, Kehaulani Kauanui, April Henderson, Noelani Goodyear-Kaopua, Heather Waldroup, and Pam Kido—about lived experiences of roots and routes. To do justice to these complex dynamics we need something a bit different from the post-colonial theorizing of Appadurai or even Gupta and Ferguson, crucial though their critiques have been. The opposition between colonial fixity and post-colonial mobility, between indigenous roots and diasporic routes, can't be naturalized, or seen as a progression, a before-after scenario. When reckoning with traveling natives, if I can call them that, in the Pacific, this sort of categorization breaks down. One encounters a range of attachments to land and place combined with old/new traditions of indigenous cosmopolitanism.

RB: In our conversations together, you have referred to the work of Stuart Hall on the articulation of cultural elements. Could you elaborate on what you find interesting about Hall's concept and how it relates to your comments here regarding the Pacific?

JC: The politics of articulation for Stuart Hall is, of course, an updating of Gramsci. It understands frontier-effects, the lining up of good and bad guys or insiders and outsiders on one side or another of a line, as tactical. Instead of rigid confrontations—us and them, civilized and primitive, bourgeois and proletarian, white and black, men and women, West and Third World—one sees continuous struggles over a terrain, portions of which are captured by different alliances, hooking up particular elements in different ways. There's a lot of middle ground and many political and cultural positions which are not firmly anchored on one side or the other but, instead, are contested and up for grabs.

Articulation suggests discourse or speech. But more importantly, it refers to connections, joints. Something that's articulated or hooked together can also be unhooked, disarticulated. So that when you consider a cultural formation as an articulated ensemble it does not allow you to prefigure it on an organic model, the notion of a living, persistent body, continuous and growing through time. An articulated ensemble is more like a cyborg, or a political coalition. While the elements and positions are historically given and sometimes quite persistent, there is no eternal or natural shape to their configuration. This kind of an ensemble is made up of structuring elements hooked onto elements of another structure, often in unexpected ways.

To me, this offers a very useful way of thinking about cultural transformation and the apparent coming and going of traditional forms. When Jean-Marie Tjibaou, the Kanak independence leader, asserts in an interview that the Bible does not belong to white people he is detaching and rearticulating elements of European and Melanesian traditions. The creation of unexpected politico-religious ensembles, often in moments of colonial stress, is what first fascinated me about the region. There are elements of Christianity to which people attached themselves and their societies rather easily, and there were other elements that they rejected or transformed. In part this was a matter of processing the new through ongoing traditional structures. But the continuity of indigenous societies has been more uneven. Since local traditions were often violently disrupted, and inasmuch as new modes of individualism and universalism have restructured bodies, societies, and spaces, the traditions that persist are best seen as original articulations of heterogeneous elements, old and new, indigenous and foreign.

In articulation theory, the whole question of authenticity or inauthenticity is set aside. It's assumed that cultural forms will be made, unmade, and remade. Communities can and must reconfigure themselves, drawing selectively on re-membered pasts. The relevant question is always a political one: Can they convince and coerce insiders and outsiders, often in power-charged and unequal situations, to accept the articulation? This to me is a more realistic way of talking about what is often termed cultural invention. As people in the Pacific know, the question of the invention of tradition is a highly disputed one. Much smoke has been generated as well as a certain amount of light. But a lot of what is referred to as invention could be rethought in terms of the politics of articulation, bypassing a lot of unfruitful impasses. It seems to me we are on much more concrete, because more dynamic, historical grounds. The whole notion of custom looks quite different when seen this way. The question of what is borrowed from here or there, what is lost and rediscovered in new situations can be discussed within the realm of normal political/cultural activity.

Articulation theory does have problems; you can only go so far with it. You can get to a point where every cultural form, every structure or restructuration, every connection and disconnection, has a fundamental contingency as if, at any moment, anything were possible. That is, in fact, a misreading of Hall on articulation. He is quite clear that the articulations, the possible connections and disconnections are constrained at any historical moment. And indeed, certain forms and antagonisms persist over long periods. Yet the enduring power of structuring forces such as Christianity, capitalism, or traditional kinship, can't be understood except as they work through specific cultural ensembles and political blocs. And these are never guaranteed, but actively sustained and potentially contested.

When thinking, as one must in the Pacific, of differently articulated sites of indigeneity, one of the enduring constraints in the mix will always be landedness, the power of place (which includes, of course, a lot of ocean). This is a fundamental component of contemporary neo-tribal, First Nations identifications. Many people live where they have always lived, even as the habitat around them has gone through violent transformations. While the scale of "tribal" and "national" existence has altered dramatically, and as people live exiled from ancestral places, they sustain a yearning, an active memory of habitat. This grounding offers a sense of depth and continuity running through the colonial, the post- and neo-colonial ruptures and attachments that have come with Christianization, governmental control, modern technology, schooling, commercial commodities, tourism and so on.

Land/habitat signifies a persistent and continuous base of political and cultural operations. Articulation theory, which sees everything as potentially realigned, cut and mixed, has difficulty with this material nexus of continuity. When a community has been living on an island for more than a thousand years, it's not enough to say that their claims to identity with a place are historical strategies of opposition and coalition in struggles with neighbors, with colonizing or world-systemic forces. It may be useful to say these things. People aren't, in fact, always attached to a habitat in the same ways, over the centuries. Communities change. The land alters. Senses of place are continuously rearticulated. And yet...this historical sense of interacting places doesn't capture the identity of ancestors with a mountain, for as long as anyone remembers and plausibly far beyond that. Indigenous myths and genealogies change, connect and reach out, but always in relation to an old and enduring spatial nexus.

I've found that when importing the work of Stuart Hall, Paul Gilroy, or Avtar Brah into the Pacific I've been made sharply aware of the diasporic Caribbean, British post-colonial, histories that lie behind it. There needs to be a significant adaptation to a different space. And I think this provincialization of theory as a condition for its travel and translation in new contexts is crucial for a really cross-cultural, cultural studies.

RB: You referred, before the interview, to an experience from your early research in the Pacific that gets at some of this.

JC: It has to do with articulated indigenous spaces. When I was writing the Leenhardt book, *Person and Myth*, I traveled in New Caledonia. I was taken around for a few days by Jean-Marie Tjibaou, who at that time, 1978, was just coming into prominence as a leader of the Kanak movement. He took me to Hienghène in the north of the island which was his home area. He had left for more than twenty years, to be trained as a Catholic priest. Now, when his clan was moving to occupy expropriated ancestral lands, he had returned as an activist.

In New Caledonia you have steep green valleys, with mountainous outcroppings. The traditional villages often occupy small hills with symbolic trees, palms and special plants dispersed in a very beautiful, orderly way.

We were in one of these villages reclining on the lawn, talking and just feeling comfortable looking out through the trees. Earlier I had been in several of the village houses, concrete structures mostly bare inside with perhaps a few newspaper clippings stuck haphazardly on the wall. I was puzzled and asked Tjibaou: "Look at this village, beautifully set in this valley, everything so aesthetically laid out. Yet inside the houses it's bare...."

We talked it over, agreeing that here, after all, people don't spend a lot of time indoors. Then suddenly my guide made a sweep with his hand that took in the village, the valley and the mountains: *Mais, c'est ça la maison.* But that's the house.

Tjibaou's sweep of the hand—including so much in his Kanak house—expressed a deep sense of being rooted in a village and a valley. This feeling of belonging, of being in scale with the world, was fundamental to Tjibaou's hope that Kanaks might find ways to feel *a'l'aise*, at home, in the twenty-first century. And as I've read more of Tjibaou's political, ethnographic, and personal writings—now collected in a superb volume, *La Présence canaque*—I've begun to think his gesture was taking in even more. Beyond the Hienghène Valley he certainly included New Caledonia and the Loyalty Islands where an articulated "Kanak" identity was emerging in political struggle. And did he also embrace the Pacific sea of islands—a wider world of cultural exchanges and alliances which were critical for Tjibaou's thinking about independence as inter-dependence? And France—whose religion and civilization, for better and worse, still contribute to the Kanak house? And...in a distinctive Kanak articulation...the world?

5. Interviewer: Yoshinobu Ota
Santa Cruz, Spring 2002

YO: When I entered graduate school in 1978 to
continue pursuing anthropology, one of the books that
captured my attention was Dell Hymes' *Reinventing
Anthropology*. In particular, I felt empowered when I
read Hymes' "Introduction," in which he stated, citing
R.G. Collingwood, that "one person's general anthropology need not be another's." This call for perspec-
tivism has stayed with me to this day. Your work, *The
Predicament of Culture*, similarly appealed to me
because it invited me to think more critically about
taken-for-granted assumptions and categories in
anthropology. I often wonder how this critical

genealogy has emerged in anthropology, a genealogy of which I would like to think I am a part, however marginal. Now, I am struggling to connect—you might prefer to say, "translate"—this critical genealogy with the intellectual development in the late '60s in Japan. My effort in translating your work is a step toward this struggle.

Being a historian with a great deal of interest in literature and anthropology, you have mentioned in your previous interviews that works of E.P. Thompson and Raymond Williams were very important to you in your intellectual formation. In the late '60s and early '70s as you went through graduate school, what aspects of anthropology—as exemplified in what constellation of texts—captured your imagination? What sort of texts and events were influential in formulating your critical thinking in anthropology?

JC: Of course, my Ph.D. was in history, and most of my closest friends were historians; I was a marginal participant in the anthropology scene at Harvard. As a graduate student I did not know—at least initially— that I would be writing in close dialogue with socio-cultural anthropology throughout my career. And while I may not be a "proper" anthropologist, I've certainly become part of anthropology, at least in its borderlands. But that relationship was all in the future. At Harvard, most of my reading was in history. I saw the work of people like E.P. Thompson or Eric Hobsbawm as cultural history (though we didn't yet have the term), as much as social and economic history. Many rather complex issues of "ethnographic" representation were central to Thompson, as he tried to evoke a whole way of life for English working people. He wrote about daily life, religion, craft rituals, local traditions, and much more. But of course he was tracking what he called a "whole way of conflict" rather than a functional unity. There was tension and rupture, there was class struggle and transformation in the middle of his rich cultural analysis. I'm sure that those ideas persisted in my thinking as I grappled with anthropological ideas of culture, especially when colonial contact histories took center stage.

What was I reading in anthropology at that time? Well, you mentioned *Reinventing Anthropology* edited by Dell Hymes. That was an important book. We all read it: for example, Laura Nader's advice to "study up," and Bob Scholte on a "reflexive and critical" anthropology. Everything in that book was part of our discourse, so much so that we sometimes forgot to reference it. Among the classics, I remember reading Malinowski and also his scandalous field diary. I guess I was part of a generation that, from the outset, read Malinowski in light of the diary and its revelations. I didn't read a lot of Clifford Geertz at that time, although he later became a very important influence. Another thing in the air was the founding of the "Cultural Survival" project by Pia and David Maybury-Lewis. I attended some of their early meetings at Harvard.

But I'm having difficulty making these influences add up to anything coherent. What was pervasive and in the air was a relentless questioning of anthropological orthodoxies. The anthropology students I knew were asking: "What is anthropology?" "What is it good for?" "How is it related to (neo) colonialism?" "How can we responsibly represent other peoples and cultures?" After the Hymes collection and after the debates that Gerald Berreman and others brought into prominence around the anthropologist's involvement in the Vietnam war, nothing was taken for granted. Another book which had a lot to do with questioning the epistemology and politics of established anthropology—a book not much discussed today but which influenced me a lot—was Stanley Diamond's *In Search of the Primitive*. Diamond placed anthropology in a subversive Western intellectual history—Rousseau, Marx, and Lévi-Strauss were its mainstream—a critical utopianism. He derived a radical perspective through a concept of "the primitive," an alter-ego to "civilization," and a resource for cultural criticism. That made a big impact, and it's a perspective that would be developed, with somewhat more irony and less romanticism perhaps, in my later work, as well as in the writings of George Marcus and Michael Fischer. In my own formation, this kind of cultural critique went together with the "ethnopoetics" of writers like Dennis Tedlock and Jerome Rothenberg.

These were the mid-'70s—and of course "the '60s" lasted into the '70s—a time of radical cultural visions. Many critical currents were present, some of which, like feminism, I would engage seriously only later. I went to Paris to do research on the history of French anthropology, and I stayed for two years. That would be about 1973-75. There I came into contact with a lot of new influences: among them, of course, French structuralism and poststructualism. I attended Foucault's lectures at the Collège de France (*La Société Punitive*), and I made contact with Michel Leiris and a host of writers and scholars little known in the United States. My friend Jean Jamin, now editor of *L'Homme*, was then sharing digs with Leiris in the rather chilly basement of the Musée de l'Homme. He opened many doors for me. We'd have coffee with Leiris in the atmospheric Museum restaurant, Le Totem, and talk about Mauss, Lévy-Bruhl, Griaule, Schaeffner, Paulme, Métraux, Bataille, Césaire… Much of this found its way into *The Predicament of Culture*. It's ironic, in fact, that when the book was translated, French readers who expected a product of *le postmodernisme Americain* found so much of themselves.

YO: The first work of yours I read is the article on Maurice Leenhardt, the one entitled "Fieldwork, Reciprocity, and the Making of Ethnographic Texts" in the British journal, *Man* (1980). I basically picked up the following two points from reading it: (1) a possibility for collaboration between an anthropologist and the local people, something that might, one day, turn into "Melanesian anthropology;" and (2) a focus on a transformation of the New Caledonian culture, as the term "living culture" from Michel Leiris seems to summarize it. In addition, these two points had come from your reading of works by an evangelist-missionary-ethnographer rather than a professional anthropologist. I interpreted this article as your saying that these are the things that anthropologists cannot afford to neglect. I then went to the southern Ryukyus to do fieldwork. When I came back to Ann Arbor, everyone was talking about "On Ethnographic Authority" in the journal, *Representations* (1983). Could you talk a little bit about that *Man* article on Leenhardt, and its relation to "On Ethnographic Authority" since the *Man* article was not included in *The Predicament of Culture*?

JC: "On Ethnographic Authority" was actually written in 1981, just a year or so after the article you mentioned on Leenhardt. In fact it flows directly from it. A major idea I derived from the experience of a liberal missionary was an explicit recognition of multiple authorship in ethnographic texts. Leenhardt, as a part of the Protestant evangelical project, elicited extensive vernacular writing from his Melanesian converts. He asked them to record their traditions and also to reflect on their whole life experience. Some of these texts were reprinted and translated in his later scholarly collections, and they were re-processed and rethought throughout his *oeuvre*.

This rather open-ended experience of writing and cultural interpretation made me question the notion of the "informant" as the uniquely oral source for cultural knowledge first written down (and then written up) by the visiting ethnographer. I started to see the whole process of ethnographic text-making as dialogical and multiply authored. One would have difficulty deriving the argument of "On Ethnographic Authority" from a classic monograph of, say, Margaret

Mead or Malinowski or Evans-Prichard, because, although one can glimpse the authority and the agency of their indigenous interlocutors (especially in Malinowski's extensive textual citations), one does not see native authority ever quite in the mode of writing. But if you dictate a myth or legend to an ethnographer, if you interpret the meaning of a festival, aren't you inscribing it? In fact, an "informant" produces many of the functions of writing even though he or she may not be the one actually using a pen. So the Leenhardt work opened up the whole question of various forms, relationships, and moments of the inscription process, a process that no longer fit into the progression: oral to literate, something unwritten that's textualized by the executive hand and function of the anthropologist.

I had to recognize a much more multi-leveled, multiply inflected sequence, which doesn't stop with the text of a published ethnography, but includes the question of reinscribing ethnographies after publication. And this points toward the "repatriation" of ethnographic texts by indigenous peoples, a direction already present in "On Ethnographic Authority," especially in the footnotes, where I talked about some of the recycled textual collections of James Walker. In the early twentieth century Walker collected an enormous number of Lakota texts, written and transcribed by various hands, which are now being used by contemporary Lakotas as part of contemporary indigenous literature and history. The same is true of "salvage" collections in many places. Recently I've been following the "second life" of the linguistic and

ethnographic compilations of A.L. Kroeber's generation in California, as California Indians reconnect with
tradition and rewrite their history. Writing clearly
doesn't begin with the moment of ethnographic
inscription nor does it end with the moment of publication. "Writing culture" is a more open-ended social
and political process.

In retrospect it seems a bit strange that I
should have derived this notion of writing from the
work of a missionary, rather than, say, from Derrida
(whose expanded concept of writing did exert an influence). But maybe not so strange.

We're now in a position to see that missionary
work in many places—the Pacific offers especially
good examples—was part of a chain of resignifications.
The moment of so-called conversion inflected
complex transformational processes that would
produce unexpected results. Melanesian Christianities
are not European Christianities. Many of the early
anti-colonial independence leaders in the Pacific were
priests or pastors. The gospel sown by missionaries
like Leenhardt, was reprocessed by their "converts,"
and the endlessly translated Word thus got involved
with some unorthodox local loops and combinations.
This is an ongoing story.

YO: Perhaps, it might be interesting to begin, again,
from elsewhere, in a field other than anthropology. In
my reading, as one who reads your work on
"Ethnographic Surrealism" from a perspective of non-
specialist on the French avant-garde scene of the
inter-war period, I must confess that I have read it

through the prism of some of your later works that highlight a concept of articulation. To be more precise, I see an idea of recombination and recoding found in surrealism (widely defined as you have done in that piece) as akin to articulation, which of course I understand comes from a different intellectual genealogy. Perhaps my reading is one-sided, but I have felt empowered, since your intellectual direction is open to emergent "Third-World modernisms," exemplified by a chapter on Aimé Césaire. This idea of "Third-World modernism" seems to raise a question of agency: who deploys recombination and recoding? I might be misled by my own desire for a smooth narrative of progression, but would you locate even in "Ethnographic Surrealism"—a product of your critical rereading of a period of decentering the West through encounters with the unfamiliar—your interest in native agency?

JC: The notions of recombination and recoding are there in surrealism, as you say; and the notion of juxtaposition, which I connect with the practice of collage in artistic practice, is reminiscent of articulation, which I use in my recent work and which is emergent in *Routes*. Certainly these notions are present in *The Predicament of Culture*. What I think is not there or, at least, not yet sufficiently, is the political dimension of all this recombination, recoding, or collage. It's still a cultural/aesthetic notion, which does not yet have, as in articulation theory, a clear idea of combinations and transformations as part of particular political strategies under specific moments and regimes of power. While this emphasis emerges more toward the end of *The Predicament of Culture*, it is not there yet in the "Ethnographic Surrealism" chapter. I did attempt a certain amount of revisionism with respect to that essay. In particular, I was unhappy with the "Paris-centeredness" of it all, leading in 1990 to a re-collaged version. This brought into prominence the Third World modernist intellectuals like Aimé Césaire, Léopold Senghor, Alejo Carpentier, and Wifredo Lam, who were traveling through Paris on trajectories that made Paris a kind of critical way-station, a moment in what Edouard Glissant, the theorist of Caribbean *creolité*, would call *détour* and *retour*. Paris was a *détour* for Third-World intellectuals, who adopted elements of surrealism while indigenizing it or localizing it in non-Western historical predicaments.

In *The Predicament of Culture*, as you say, this emergent awareness was crystalized in the figure of Aimé Césaire. I came to Césaire through Michel Leiris, who was both a surrealist—or sometimes a surrealist—and an ethnologist. Leiris kept the two practices separate but, let's say, near-by. Cultural politics—a notion of culture-in-transformation, in conflict, working through impurities to produce a new dynamism and a mode of resistance to colonial hegemonies—this vision of culture is very much part of Césaire's work, of course. And it's also central to Leiris' ethnological vision as it took shape in the post-war period of anti-colonial rebellions. Leiris wrote, in the early '50s, an essay "L'Ethnographe devant le colonialisme" which I think is still one of the best essays on that issue. So the "Ethnographic Surrealism" essay eventually led me to engage with non-European trajectories of cultural poetics and critique which one can't think of as simply emanations of Paris, or New York or Berlin. Diverse Third-World modernisms emerged from rather complicated engagements and disengagements, travels to, through, and out of, those First-World places.

YO: As one of the translators of *The Predicament of Culture* I am curious to know how you might locate your work in 2002. In March a Japanese translation of your more recent work, *Routes*, became available; for this reason many Japanese readers will encounter two of your works in a reverse chronological order within this year. This fact, I think, might produce a reading of *The Predicament of Culture* quite different from the ones dominant in the United States: For example, an interpretation that *The Predicament of Culture* signals a "literary turn" in anthropology might be less salient than another reading that it creates a space for tribal modernities, presents-becoming-futures. How would you characterize the trajectory of your thought as you reflect on it, here and now?

JC: I'm glad that these two books are appearing in Japan in a reverse order. Doesn't every author want his/her work to take on a new life when translated? Having the books read out of sequence is an excellent way to produce new meanings: Japan in the twenty-first century is hardly the context of reception that guided my writing. And, yes, I would like to think that after reading *Routes* it would be more difficult to construe *The Predicament of Culture* as essentially a book about the "literary turn" in anthropology or as primarily about textualization—though it is, of course, partly about these things. Looked at from the perspective of what is emergent in the book, *Predicament* is less concerned with textual form than with cultural process, with projects of transformation and with opening up—displacing—colonial authority in ways that go beyond simply a matter of who writes the ethnographic text, and in what form. It's primarily about discourse. And discourse, of course, is a concept that has much broader, "cultural" application, both institutionally and politically, than writing as usually understood.

YO: I was born in Hokkaido, the land of the Ainu, the indigenous people of Japan. Until recently they were said to be assimilated completely to Japanese society. When I returned to Japan to teach in 1989, I could not help noticing the presence of Ainus in the media more than any time I could remember: the Ainu people were struggling to regain their language, to construct their own museums, and even to offer educational tourism. In 1994 the first Ainu person was elected a member of the Diet. But, the Japanese government has not recognized the Ainu as indigenous, despite the fact that in 1997 the government lost a trial (over the construction of a dam) in which the verdict clearly defined them in those terms. Like many similar peoples around the world, Ainu have been building a global network; so the emergence of indigenous people in Japanese society is not an isolated phenomenon. Could you say something about the emergence of indigenous peoples as voices to be reckoned with in the contemporary world? Since the last chapter of *The Predicament of Culture* is about the Mashpee trial, does this chapter point toward the direction of your more recent work?

JC: The fact that in 1989 the Ainu were more publicly active than ever before is part of a global phenomenon. Fifteen or twenty years ago the word "indigenous" simply was not on our agendas, was not something we needed to be talking about. Of course we knew there were native peoples: Aboriginals, First Nations, tribal peoples. We knew they were struggling, dying, surviving, transforming. All of this was happening, but not in relation to a global category of the indigenous, in its present articulated form. There was not yet a United Nations Year of Indigenous Peoples, and we didn't have a whole world of NGO's connected with indigenous politics, hooking up local/global environmental coalitions, and a variety of Fourth-World institutions. This new public sphere is a feature of the last twenty years, and in my current work I'm struggling to account for its old and new roots and routes in a comparative way.

I first confronted these complexities, as you suggest, in 1978 when I attended a trial in which the Mashpee—a community of Indians on Cape Cod—had to prove that they were a real Indian tribe. It seemed to me that they lost in court because they came up against certain categories, a number of them anthropological, which made it very hard to demonstrate their existence as a continuously existing people. Their historical experience, over several centuries of conquest, colonization, and partial assimilation, had been discontinuous and embattled in ways that could not be accommodated by prevailing notions of identity and cultural continuity. As a critical historian of anthropology I was interested in problematizing just these categories. But what I needed to understand more positively, what the categories obscured, was the very complex historical persistence of the Mashpee. These Indians don't fit most of the models of what an authentic tribal group should look like, yet they unmistakably do exist and are a part of a multiply-sited phenomenon, the emergence of locally, regionally, nationally, even internationally connected worlds of indigenous life. For example, Mashpee people had traveled to Hawai'i and all over. This was held against them in the trial, because it made them seem less rooted and therefore less authentic. I had to learn that this sort of movement, in-and-out-of-a-place, across very uneven landscapes, could be very much part of native life. This led me into the whole paradigm of "routes" articulated with "roots," that formed the basis of my next book. I was trying to come to terms with emergent and multiply-scaled performances and translations of indigenous life in the late twentieth and now early twenty-first century, experiences for which the categories that had been given to me by a general anthropological common sense did not seem adequate. So now I'm trying to sort out the differently articulated, but comparable, experiences of contemporary

Native American, First Nation's Canadian, Pan-Mayan, Arctic, Australian, and Pacific Islands indigenous movements.

YO: The complex trajectories of indigenous modernity in the contemporary world have also forced anthropologists to think about the nature of ethnographic practices. Sometimes, the indigenous "coming-into-representation," to borrow a phrase from Stuart Hall, has complicated relationships between individual anthropologists and indigenous peoples: for example, the debate surrounding the "invention of tradition" in the Pacific and South America; and closer to my current interest, the case of Rigoberta Menchú and David Stoll. Could you comment on this problematization of "anthropological authority" in the light of indigenous cultural and political mobilization?

JC: I've always felt that possibly the most significant change in redefining and repositioning the authority of anthropologists in the late twentieth century is the simple fact that the so-called objects of their study, their "informants," are increasingly critical readers of their work. Anthropologists now operate in domains of publicly contested authority. And the presence of the new indigenous politics, of locally mobilized communities, has made life more difficult, no doubt about that. Anthropologists are greeted with a newly-public suspicion. In some contexts fieldwork is simply off-limits. In others, different forms of alliance and shared authority have emerged. Some scholars react with anger and bitterness to the changes, saying they undermine the ground of a disengaged science, the very possibility of objectivity. I see their point, especially in polarized situations where research is reduced to simple advocacy. But there are many intermediate accommodations, in practice. Moreover, as a historian of the discipline, I don't think anthropological research, particularly in the field, has ever been disengaged. And I'm not sure objectivity, or scientific "freedom," was ever something anthropology had to lose. At least since Paul Rabinow's hard-nosed *Reflections on Fieldwork in Morocco* we've had to confront the limits, trade-offs, negotiated reciprocities, and the sometimes violent push-and-pull of fieldwork. And the geo-political conditions that had made possible the kind of science for which some now express a certain nostalgia, are finished, at least in many parts of the world. The decolonization movements of the 1950s and '60s have had an uneven, but I think cumulatively irreversible effect. So today ethnographers (also archaeologists and linguists) negotiate different relations of access, authority, inscription and reciprocity.

In the case of Rigoberta Menchú and David Stoll, for example, or the well-known arguments in the Pacific and elsewhere about the "invention of tradition," we see a freezing of roles, in which anthropologists are pushed into the corner of being the objective witness who judges the truth of indigenous claims, adjudicating the authenticity of the culture in question: what is really traditional, what is made up. In relation to Menchú, Stoll plays the part of scientific wet blanket, producing empirical refutations of the "merely political" native. Inasmuch as two positions of authority are reified here, that of the indigenous activist and the scientific reporter, this is dangerous for anthropology. It blocks the diverse forms of complicity and alliance that have always made good ethnographic collaboration possible, and it reinforces a native stereotype of the anthropologist. I don't think that one needs to give up skepticism and a commitment to empirically verifiable truth (when something like conclusive evidence does actually exist) while still staying engaged with the many avenues of truth-telling in cross-cultural interpretation and resisting moves to confine anthropology to a narrow scientism. There is, as I've said, a lot of middle ground.

YO: So the agendas of the anthropologist and the indigenous communities need not be contradictory and confrontational?

JC: No, not necessarily. There are plenty of examples of collaborative work being done by anthropologists with mobilized native communities, where scientific and indigenous projects can overlap, while agreeing to differ on other matters. A couple of cases from Alaska come to mind. Archaeologists Aron Crowell and Amy Steffian, along with various academic/Native colleagues, have recently published an exemplary book, *Looking Both Ways: Heritage and Identity of the Alutiiq People*. It records a long process of collaborative work with Alutiiq elders and activists, including their co-editor Gordon Pullar, linking together research agendas. Where worldviews collide, an openness to different stories, a respectful live-and-let-live attitude is sustained. Another example is the work of anthropologist Ann Fienup-Riordan: an evolving series of books about Yup'ik Eskimos, works that increasingly foreground their own collaborative structure. Working closely with local authorities she helped develop an extraordinary exhibition of masks which opened first in Yup'ik communities and then traveled to major Alaskan cities and in the lower 48 states. Local reception of the project was crucial, but not exclusive. The masks and their stories meant different things to different audiences, as Fienup-Riordan shows in her recent co-authored book, *Hunting Tradition*. These are examples in which serious ethnographic, historical, archaeological scholarship has been combined with indigenous agendas to produce compelling accounts of local traditions and emergent cultural formations. David Hurst-Thomas, in *Skull Wars*, his recent history of American archaeology's often exploitative history of relations with indigenous peoples, ends with similar examples of collaborative work. I don't mean to suggest that there are any guaranteed, "post-colonial" relations for an anthropology that is still enmeshed in unequal power relations. Only that notions of scientific authority can, in practice, be re-negotiated in specific, and more egalitarian, alliances.

YO: You write in *The Predicament of Culture* of an indigenous "present-becoming-future," and I've found this useful in thinking about the complex trajectories of tribal peoples as they negotiate their existence in modernity. As I read *The Predicament of Culture* again in the mid-'90s, I linked this phrase in my mind with an idea proposed in *Blues People* by Leroi Jones/Amiri Baraka, the "changing same." He's writing of Duke Ellington's jazz as something one can trace the roots of yet that sounds fresh. I would be very interested in hearing you talk a bit about this concept, "present-becoming-future"? To me, it's very different from approaches often developed from the "invention of tradition" idea.

JC: The phrase "present-becoming-future" is, of course, an attempt to get tribal folks out of an almost automatic association with the past. And the idea of a "changing same" is probably what a lot of indigenous neo-traditionalists are interested in, a sense of *longue durée*, of a continuity of belonging, with room for a lot of change. It's important to keep in mind that this "present-becoming-future" is complexly connected to some very old "pasts." There are affiliations, roots, to ancient traditions, and especially to ancient places, specific locations in the land, which have an enduring quality. But enduring and transformation are never in opposition; the backward connection isn't about nostalgia in the sense of returning to something lost. People are always "looking both ways," (as the Alutiiq project title suggests) to the past and to the future. Reaching back in indigenous movements to recover lost traditions, to reclaim languages which are threat-ened, to make legal claims on expropriated land, to repatriate human remains and works of art (which have been traveling on a long detour, through museums and universities in cities of the dominant societies); all of these movements of return are movements forward: the indigenous present-becoming-future.

One of the ways that anthropologists and historians have understood such processes is under the rubric of "invention." But the idea has run into trouble with mobilized indigenous people for both good and bad reasons. The bad reasons have had to do with identity politics in an exclusivist sense, with policing the borders of "insider" knowledge. The good reasons concern the inevitable semantic weight the word "invention" carries, the idea that something invented is something made up, in some sense, "fake," or not fully authentic. You can't use the language of invention without getting involved with the language of authenticity. But I think this almost always leads us into locking horns, into rather fruitless arguments from prescribed positions. The kinds of collaborative, translational practices I was referring to, and the kind of historical thinking I have been struggling toward myself, need to go beyond all-or-nothing attitudes to authenticity, cultural purity, and ascribed authority (whether indigenous or academic).

YO: You have mentioned in previous interviews that you find intriguing the timing of decolonization in the Pacific and that you see the "uneven process of decolonization" as the "hinge of your work," a political process taking new forms as capitalism transforms itself into post-Fordism. The idea of sovereignty becomes complicated in the face of the declining control of nations.

I think a place like Japan is still entangled in the uneven process of decolonization. I say this because decolonization, when equated with demilitarization after World War II, did not register as such for the Japanese. What made matters worse is that Japan's entry into the Cold War regime effectively occulted it from the Japanese consciousness. Consequently, decolonization for the colonizer—the issue is relevant both for the colonized and colonizer, as historian Taichiro Mitani says—did not surface until the regime ended in the late '80s. In the case of Japan, the ex-colonized came into representation only in the early '90s, demanding to be heard by the Japanese people: so-called "comfort women" and colonial laborers coerced into work in the mines and at factories, to name just two cases now contested in the courts. The histories of Japanese colonialism represented in school text books remain contested by formerly colonized nations in East Asia. The people who were once seen as nothing but a part of the war memory come back to voice their demands for reparation.

Decolonization is, indeed, a very "uneven process": I heard from a Mayan leader that decolonization, far from being something in the past, has not yet started in Guatemala. In a similar vein decolonization, thought to belong to the past and to other places, caught up with the Japanese at the height of economic prosperity in the early '90s. I approach Guatemalan Mayan movements—emerging from the experience of genocide—from a perspective that links them with the demands made to the Japanese government by ex-

colonial subjects. I see this unfinished project of decolonization as the key term which links the concerns
Japanese society cannot ignore for constructing meaningful relations with Asian countries in the future with
those the Guatemalan society cannot ignore for
constructing a more democratic Guatemala out of the
history of genocide now documented in two important
post-Peace Accord reports. As a Japanese anthropologist who studies Guatemalan society, I cannot help
creating this juxtaposition of the two countries,
twisted out of time and space.

Could you comment on the process of decolonization? In the United States it may have very
different effects from what has been occurring in the
Pacific, Guatemala, and Japan.

JC: What you say about different temporalities of
decolonization is very interesting. It's especially
important to think of decolonization not as an event,
but as unfinished, uneven processes. There is a
tendency to say that decolonization is something that
happened in the '50s and perhaps the early '60s. This
view highlights the political independence of various
colonies during that period rather than an ongoing set
of struggles and re-positionings occurring not only at
political-economic levels but also at many cultural
levels within a variety of societies. If one assumes that
decolonization was an important event which
happened in the '50s, then what followed can only be
its containment by neo-colonialism. This is a very
common Left critique which I think has a significant
element of truth in it. Neo-colonialism sets in, and the

great liberatory appeal that the generation of postwar decolonizers like Césaire or Ho-Chi-Minh expressed is bought off, channeled into what is now called globalization. But is the history really so linear?

In the current moment—call it globalization, late capitalism, postmodernity—everything seems more flexible, Americanized, overdetermined, simultaneously ordered and chaotic. My view is that the forces unleashed by decolonization movements after the Second World War have not been contained or defeated. Something fundamental took hold there and has continued to generate contestations in systems of hegemonic power. But the last fifty years clearly show that decolonization does not guarantee liberation; it does not build to some complete, global overthrow of systems of domination. Capital and empire don't simply wither away—far from it. But the historical processes active in the world do produce aspirations to liberation and partial displacements of power, opening up, as we've been discussing, political spaces for indigenous peoples who were expected to die, who had no futures in previous historical imaginings. So when forced to periodize I fall back on formulas that express this tension, like "post-/neo-colonial."

Speaking now of the United States, decolonization (always in tension with new forms of governmentality) has been active in educational institutions such as the ones I have known since the '60s. I'm thinking of a dramatic opening up of the curriculum to non-European works and of the arrival in our universities of more diverse faculty and students. These are processes which are far from complete, processes that have not revolutionized our universities but that in significant ways have transformed them. A certain containment by so-called "identity politics" and a liberal managed diversity are very much part of the story. But not the whole story. In any event, few would want to go back to the prior condition of homogeneity. That's the ambiguous history I've been part of and that had do to with the ways decolonization began to bite in the United States. Feminism was a critical part of the process, related to, but not identical with, decolonization. It has to do with the specific history of the '60s and its aftermath in the United States, the ambiguous emergence of so-called multiculturalism—in both critical and governmental strains—the consequences of which are as yet undetermined. It's an open-ended story—at least I hope so. *The Predicament of Culture* was part of this history. But read now, in Japan, it becomes part of a different moment which you, better than I, can understand.

YO: If indeed the effect of decolonization is still felt in the various discussions of multiculturalism and, to be a little more general, of the politics of identity, in the United States, could you talk a bit about that? How do you approach the ethnically mobilized, identity-based movements? In my work in Guatemala I always find myself disagreeing with the point often made by critics of Mayan movements that Mayans do nothing but assert essential and fundamental differences, with the result that national unity can never be achieved. This seems to be a case of colonial discourse surviving into the twenty-first century.

JC: In the United States and Europe, we have seen a widespread reaction against the anti-colonial disruptions that were only partially contained by the misleading name "multiculturalism." The whole process is reduced to a narrow form of so-called identity politics, where people are said to ghettoize themselves inside essentialized or absolutist notions of identity, claims of victimhood, self-congratulatory nationalisms, and so forth. Wider forms of citizenship, or oppositional politics, become impossible. Diversity appears as little more than postmodern divide-and-rule. I am only half persuaded by this kind of critique: multiculturalism as divisive identity politics. The critique does name real political problems of coalition building. But its diagnosis of their causes is simplistic, and unexamined universalisms are often assumed to provide the cure. I don't think the dismissal of identity politics really accounts for the full range of reactions, the unruly forces that decolonization has set in motion.

We always need to distinguish between ideological identity and pragmatic identity. The same people who draw a hard line around peoplehood and culture in one moment, will be involved in some very complex crossings and negotiations of those very boundaries in another. Fredrik Barth, some time ago, taught us that ethnic difference is border work, articulated in contexts of entanglement and similarity. People are connected-in-difference, if only because everybody is economically and culturally linked. There is no way to cut oneself off, and this goes for the most isolated island in the Pacific. (Actually, it's especially true of islands, who must look outward.) So absolutist notions of identity, sovereignty, culture, community, etc. need to be seen in bifocal or multi-focal ways, not simply in terms of the identity politics that insurgent social movements often claim, and that official multiculturalisms struggle to manage, in conditions of postmodern globalization.

The kind of ethnographic work you're doing in Guatemala with Mayan movements, ambivalent participants in this simultaneously globalizing and localizing, post- and neo-colonial moment, is very important. By focusing on complex, lived experiences we begin to see the multiple strategies and often discontinuous operations of both decolonization and recolonization. I think of these indigenous movements for recognition and self-determination as conjunctural, Gramscian politics, struggles over particular pieces of cultural and economic terrain, attempts to carve out living spaces and breathing room in situations that can at best be partially controlled. It's not "revolutionary" politics in the sense of a cumulative Third-World (or Fourth-World) movement that at some point escapes, or transcends technological/industrial modernity. I do not, in any case, think of modernity, or the West, or capitalism, as unified phenomena. Nor do I think of the various identities that are reckoning with global processes as all following similar historical paths. Not necessarily. The range of actually-existing articulations is full of surprises, if one knows how to pay attention. Marshall Sahlins calls this attentiveness "anthropological enlightenment." I agree. And this is why we will always need historically-engaged ethnography—to keep us surprised, listening, receptive to emergence, peering into the shadows shed by our enlightenment. ■

Further Reading

Appiah, Kwame Anthony 2000 "Cosmopolitan Patriots." In *Cosmopolitics: Thinking and Feeling Beyond the Nation*. Pheng Cheah and Bruce Robbins, eds., pp. 91-116. Minneapolis: University of Minnesota Press.

Barth, Fredrik, ed. 1969 *Ethnic Groups and Boundaries*. Boston: Little Brown.

Clifford, James 1980 "Fieldwork, Reciprocity, and the Making of Ethnographic Texts." Man 15: 518-532.

_____ 1982 *Person and Myth: Maurice Leenhardt in the Melanesian World*. Berkeley: University of California Press.

_____ 1988 *The Predicament of Culture: Twentieth Century Ethnography, Literature and Art*. Berkeley: University of California Press.

_____ 1990 "Documents: A Decomposition" In *Anxious Visions*. Sidra Stitch, ed., pp. 176-199. New York: Abberville Press.

_____ 1997 *Routes*. Cambridge, MA: Harvard University Press.

_____ 2000 "Taking Identity Politics Seriously: 'The Contradictory, Stony Ground...'" In *Without Guarantees: In Honour of Stuart Hall*. Paul Gilroy, Lawrence Grossberg and Angela McRobbie, eds., pp. 94-112. London: Verso.

Clifford, James and George Marcus, eds. 1986 *Writing Culture: The Poetics and Politics of Ethnography*. Berkeley: University of California Press.

Crowell, Aron, Amy Steffian and Gordon Pullar, eds. 2001 *Looking Both Ways: Heritage and Identity of the Alutiiq People*. Fairbanks: University of Alaska Press.

Diamond, Stanley 1974 *In Search of the Primitive*. New Brunswick: Transaction Books.

Diaz, Vicente and J. Kehaulani Kauanui, eds. 2001 "Native Pacific Cultural Studies on the Edge." *Special Issue: The Contemporary Pacific* 13 (2).

Einzig, Barbara, ed. 1998 *Thinking About Art: Conversations with Susan Hiller*. Manchester and New York: Manchester University Press.

Fienup-Riordan, Ann 1996 *The Living Tradition of Yup'ik Masks: Agayuliyararput (Our Way of Making Prayer)* Seattle: University of Washington Press.

_____ 2000 *Hunting Tradition in a Changing World: Yup'ik Lives in Alaska today*. New Brunswick, N.J.: Rutgers University Press.

Firth, Stewart 2000 "Decolonization." In *Remembrance of Pacific Pasts*. Robert Borofsky, ed. pp. 314-332. Honolulu: University of Hawaii Press.

Friedman, Jonathan 1994 *Cultural Identity and Global Process*. London: Sage.

Hau'ofa, Epeli 1993 "Our Sea of Islands." In *A New Oceania: Rediscovering Our Sea of Islands*. Eric Waddell, Vijay Naidu, and Epeli Hau'ofa, eds., pp. 2-19. Suva: School of Social and Economic Development, University of the South Pacific.

_____ 2000 "Pasts to Remember." In *Remembrance of Pacific Pasts*. Robert Borofsky, ed., pp. 453-471. Honolulu: University of Hawaii Press.

Hymes, Dell, ed. 1972 *Reinventing Anthropology*. New York: Pantheon.

Jones, Leroi 1963 *Blues People*. New York: Quill.

Leiris, Michel 1987 *Nights as Day, Days as Nights*, translated by Richard Sieburth. New York: Eridanos Press.

Said, Edward 1975 *Beginnings: Intention and Method*. New York: Basic Books.

Pratt, Mary 1992 *Imperial Eyes: Travel Writing and Transculturation*. London: Routledge.

Rabinow, Paul 1977 *Reflections on Fieldwork in Morocco*. Berkeley: University of California Press.

Sahlins, Marshall 1999 "What is Anthropological Enlightenment? Some Lessons of the Twentieth Century." *Annual Review of Anthropology* 28. Reprinted in *Culture in Practice*, pp. 501-526. Zone Books, 2000.

Thomas, David Hurst 2000 *Skull Wars: Kennewick Man, Archaeology, and the Battle for Native American Identity*. New York: Basic Books.

Thompson, E.P. 1963 *The Making of the English Working Class*. London: Victor Gollancz.

Tjibaou, Jean-Marie 1996 *La Présence kanak*. Alban Bensa and Eric Wittersheim, eds. Paris: Editions Odile Jacob.

Tomlinson, John 1999 *Globalization and Culture*. Chicago: University of Chicago Press.

Wagner, Roy 1975 *The Invention of Culture*. Engelwood Cliffs, N.J.: Prentice Hall.

Williams, Raymond 1958 *Culture and Society, 1780-1950*. New York and London: Chatto and Windus.

Look for these titles by Prickly Paradigm, and others to come: